PENGUIN BOO

A V

1. *Voices of Akenfield* Ronald Blythe
2. *The Wood* John Stewart Collis
3. *From Dover to the Wen* William Cobbett
4. *The Pleasures of English Food* Alan Davidson
5. *Through England on a Side-Saddle* Celia Fiennes
6. *Elegy Written in a Country Churchyard and Other Poems* Various
7. *A Shropshire Lad* A. E. Housman
8. *Cathedrals and Castles* Henry James
9. *Walks in the Wheat-fields* Richard Jefferies
10. *The Beauties of a Cottage Garden* Gertrude Jekyll
11. *Country Churches* Simon Jenkins
12. *A Wiltshire Diary* Francis Kilvert
13. *Some Country Houses and their Owners* James Lees-Milne
14. *The Clouded Mirror* L. T. C. Rolt
15. *Let Us Now Praise Famous Gardens* Vita Sackville-West
16. *One Green Field* Edward Thomas
17. *English Folk Songs* Ralph Vaughan Williams and A. L. Lloyd
18. *Country Lore and Legends* Jennifer Westwood and Jacqueline Simpson
19. *Birds of Selborne* Gilbert White
20. *Life at Grasmere* Dorothy and William Wordsworth

A
WILTSHIRE
DIARY

Francis
Kilvert

English 🐧 *Journeys*

PENGUIN BOOKS

Published by the Penguin Group
Penguin Books Ltd, 80 Strand, London WC2R 0RL, England
Penguin Group (USA) Inc., 375 Hudson Street, New York, New York 10014, USA
Penguin Group (Canada), 90 Eglinton Avenue East, Suite 700, Toronto, Ontario, Canada M4P 2Y3
(a division of Pearson Penguin Canada Inc.)
Penguin Ireland, 25 St Stephen's Green, Dublin 2, Ireland
(a division of Penguin Books Ltd)
Penguin Group (Australia), 250 Camberwell Road, Camberwell, Victoria 3124, Australia
(a division of Pearson Australia Group Pty Ltd)
Penguin Books India Pvt Ltd, 11 Community Centre, Panchsheel Park, New Delhi – 110 017, India
Penguin Group (NZ), 67 Apollo Drive, Rosedale, North Shore 0632, New Zealand
(a division of Pearson New Zealand Ltd)
Penguin Books (South Africa) (Pty) Ltd, 24 Sturdee Avenue, Rosebank, Johannesburg 2196, South Africa

Penguin Books Ltd, Registered Offices: 80 Strand, London WC2R 0RL, England

www.penguin.com

Selections from the Diary of the Rev. Francis Kilvert was first published in three volumes:
Volume I: 1870–1871 in 1938
Volume II: 1871–1874 in 1939
Volume III: 1874–1879 in 1940
The material for this edition was taken from a one-volume selection published in 1941
Published in Penguin Books 2009

3

Set by Rowland Phototypesetting Ltd, Bury St Edmunds, Suffolk
Printed in England by Clays Ltd, St Ives plc

978-0-141-19101-0

www.greenpenguin.co.uk

Penguin Books is committed to a sustainable future
for our business, our readers and our planet.
The book in your hands is made from paper
certified by the Forest Stewardship Council.

— 1872 —

TUESDAY, 3 SEPTEMBER

When I opened my window at Langley Burrell Rectory
this morning the first sound I heard was the tapping of
a nuthatch in an acacia. There had been a little rain
in the night but the morning was fine. At 9.20 I left
Chippenham to join the rest of the party, my mother,
Dora, and the children Katie and Monk, at 1 Prince's
Buildings, Weston, leaving my Father and Fanny alone
at Langley.

WEDNESDAY, 4 SEPTEMBER

Bathing in the morning before breakfast from a machine.
Many people were openly stripping on the sands a little
further on and running down into the sea, and I would
have done the same but I had brought down no towels
of my own.

At 7 o'clock this evening my Mother, Dora and I
walked up to Trinity Church and heard Mr Hunt preach.
During the service the lightning looked in at the windows
and shamed the gas while from the town far below came
up on the still sultry air the strains of the Italian band.

THURSDAY, 5 SEPTEMBER

I was out early before breakfast this morning bathing from the sands. There was a delicious feeling of freedom in stripping in the open air and running down naked to the sea, where the waves were curling white with foam and the red morning sunshine glowing upon the naked limbs of the bathers.

[Kilvert returns to Langley Burrell.]

MONDAY, 16 SEPTEMBER

At 6 o'clock this evening a large balloon, striped red and blue, passed over this house very high in the air, almost a mile high it was said. It looked very small and we could not see the car. There was one man in it and he kept on sending down parachutes and emptying sandbags. The balloon was rapidly travelling eastwards in a straight line, but it had previously been veering about a good deal in various currents of air, passing over the Plough before it came to us. The balloon started from Bristol where there was a great Conservative demonstration and came down at Yatesbury.

The Yatesbury people were terrified when they saw the balloon descending and some ran away and some stared. But the aeronaut could get no one to help him or catch hold of the grappling ropes to steady the balloon, so it came down bump and bounced up again. At last it was secured and packed, and the aeronaut found board and bed at the Parsonage. It was said that he had made 30 ascents before.

FRIDAY, 27 SEPTEMBER

Maria told us the story of Anne Kilvert and the cat, and the Epiphany Star. It seems that when Aunt Sophia was dying Anna thought some mutton would do her good and went to fetch some. When she came back the nurse said, 'She can't eat mutton. She's dying'. Anna put the mutton down on the floor and rushed to the bed. At that moment Aunt Sophia died and Anna turned round to see the cat running away with the mutton and the Epiphany Star shining in through the window.

WEDNESDAY, 9 OCTOBER

Mrs Haddrell showed me a brown linnet in her room and she said she had a lark 'but he makes no *charm* now'.

MONDAY, 14 OCTOBER

Last night I had a strange and horrible dream. It was one of those curious things, a dream within a dream, like a picture within a picture. I dreamt that I dreamt that Mr and Mrs Venables tried to murder me. We were all together in a small room and they were both trying to poison me, but I was aware of their intention and baffled them repeatedly. At length, Mr Venables put me off my guard, came round fondling me, and suddenly clapping his hand on my neck behind said, 'It's of no use, Mr Kilvert. You're done for'. I felt the poison beginning to work and burn in my neck. I knew it was all over and started up in fury and despair. I flew at him savagely. The scene suddenly changed to the organ loft in Hardenhuish Church. Mr Venables, seeing me coming at him, burst out at the door. Close outside the door was standing the Holy Ghost. He knocked him from the top to the bottom of the stairs, rolling over head over heels, rushed downstairs himself, mounted his horse and fled away, I after him.

This dream within a dream excited me to such a state of fury, that in the outer dream I determined to murder Mr Venables. Accordingly I lay in wait for him with a pickaxe on the Vicarage lawn at Clyro, hewed an immense and hideous hole through his head, and kicked his face till it was so horribly mutilated, crushed and disfigured as to be past recognition. Then the spirit of the dream changed. Mrs Venables became her old natural self again. 'Wasn't it enough,' she said, looking at me reproachfully, 'that you should have hewed that hole through his head, but you must go and kick his face so that I don't know him again?' At this moment, Mr Bevan, the Vicar of Hay, came in. 'Well,' he said to me, 'you *have* done it now. You have made a pretty mess of it.'

All this time I was going about visiting the sick at Clyro and preaching in Clyro Church. But I saw that people were beginning to look shy at me and suspect me of the murder which had just been discovered. I became so wretched and conscience-stricken that I could bear my remorse no longer in secret and I went to give myself up to a policeman, who immediately took me to prison where I was kept in chains. Then the full misery of my position burst upon me and the ruin and disgrace I had brought on my family. 'It will kill my father,' I cried in an agony of remorse and despair.

I knew it was no dream. This at last was a reality from which I should never awake. I had awaked from many evil dreams and horrors and found them unreal, but this was a reality and horror from which I should never awake. It was all true at last. I had committed a murder. I calculated the time. I knew the Autumn Assizes were over and I could not be tried till the Spring. 'The Assizes,' I said, 'will come on in March and I shall be hung early in April.' And at the words I saw Mrs Venables give a shudder of horror.

When I woke I was so persuaded of the reality of what I had seen and felt and done in my dreams that I felt for the handcuffs on my wrists and could not believe I was in bed at home till I heard the old clock on the stairs warn and then strike five.

Nothing now seems to me so real and tangible as that dream was, and it seems to me as I might wake up at any moment and find everything shadowy, fleeting and unreal. I feel as if life is a dream from which at any moment I may awake.

SUNDAY, 20 OCTOBER

A dark wet day. I read prayers in the morning and a Declaration of Assent to the Prayer Book and Articles on being licensed to the Curacy of Langley Burrell. I think this proclamation rather astonished the people.

THURSDAY, 24 OCTOBER

A wild wet morning. Charles Awdry of Draycot came over to call on me this afternoon, and I walked back with him as far as Cold Harbour. He told me he once said to Lord Cowley at Draycot House, 'My ancestors owned this estate when yours were peasants.' 'It is true,' Lord Cowley said. 'We are only a hundred years old.'

SUNDAY, 27 OCTOBER

I have rarely seen Langley Church and Churchyard look more beautiful than they did this morning. The weather was lovely and round the quiet Church the trees were gorgeous, the elms dazzling golden and the beeches burning crimson. The golden elms illuminated the Church and Churchyard with strong yellow light and the beeches flamed and glowed with scarlet and crimson fire like the Burning Bush. The place lay quiet in the still autumn sunshine. Then the latch of the wicket gate tinkled and pretty Keren Wood appeared coming along the Church path under the spreading boughs of the wide larch, and in the glare of yellow light the bell broke solemnly through the golden elms that stood stately round the Church.

To-day we had one of those soft, still, dreamy, golden afternoons peculiar to Autumn.

MONDAY, 28 OCTOBER

This afternoon I cleaned the harness entirely myself and sent it out smarter and brighter than it has been I think for years.

WEDNESDAY, 30 OCTOBER

Called on the Dallins, the new people at Langley Lodge, and found both Captain and Mrs Dallin were out riding.

MONDAY, 25 NOVEMBER

The old Manor House of Langley Burrell used to stand on the knoll just beyond the fishpond below the terrace walk, where an oak stands now. The new Manor House was built about 100 years ago by Robert Ashe, Rector of the Parish and Lord of the Manor, my great-great-grandfather. The stones for the new houses were hewn by an old man named Old Chit Chat. When he got his pay he would go down the ancient footpath by Pen Hills House tossing a coin with himself to see whether his belly or his back should get the benefit of his wages. If the back won the toss Old Chit Chat would toss again to give the poor belly one more chance. The game generally ended by his going to the public house.

FRIDAY, 29 NOVEMBER

The Irvingites are all in a flutter of expectation and excitement. They believe that Christ has already come and is at Glasgow working miracles.

Miss Mewburn whom I met at the Kerrys' this evening lent me a pamphlet by Edward Hine on the identity of the English nation with the ten lost tribes of Israel. It is a grand idea and an interesting and exciting surmise. We 'stared at each other with a wild surmise'. I only hope it is true. It would be a glorious truth.

Miss Mewburn went to the Agricultural Meeting at the Town Hall at Chippenham yesterday and came away furious at the patronizing manner in which the labourers were preached at and the way in which the poor old people were kept standing during the whole meeting, while *'their betters'* (?) were comfortably seated in cushioned chairs. She wished she could have lifted up her voice and borne witness against the proceedings. And I very heartily sympathize with her feelings.

MONDAY, DECEMBER MORROW

To-day we had a luncheon party to meet the Dallins. Mrs Dallin looked very nice. She was exquisitely dressed in rich black silk with loose open sleeves. Poor child, she confided to Fannie that she was very dull. Hardly anyone had been to see her.

TUESDAY, 3 DECEMBER

My thirty-third birthday.

FRIDAY, 6 DECEMBER

Dined with the Dallins at Langley Lodge. A handsome and most hospitable entertainment and a very pleasant friendly evening. Two soups, champagne and curaçao.

SUNDAY, 8 DECEMBER

The morning had been lovely, but during our singing practice after evening Church at about half past four began the Great Storm of 1872. Suddenly the wind rose up and began to roar at the Tower window and shake the panes and lash the glass with torrents of rain. It grew very dark. The storm increased and we struggled home in torrents of rain and tempests of wind so fearful that we could hardly force our way across the Common to the Rectory. All the evening the roaring S. W. wind raged more and more furious. It seemed as if the windows on the west side of the house must be blown in. The glass cracked and strained and bent and the storm shrieked and wailed and howled like multitudes of lost spirits. I went out to see where the cows were, fearing that the large elms in the Avenue might fall and crush them. The trees were writhing, swaying, rocking, lashing their arms wildly and straining terribly in the tempest but I could not see that any were gone yet. The twin firs in the orchard seemed the worst off, they gave the wind such a power and purchase, with their heavy green boughs, and their tops were swaying fearfully and bending nearly double under the tremendous strain. The moon was high and the clouds drove wild and fast across her face. Dark storms and thick black drifts were hurrying up out of the west, where the Almighty was making the clouds His chariot and walking upon the wings of the wind. Now and then the moon looked out for a moment wild and terrified through a savage rent in the storm.

The cows were safe in the cowyard and the door shut, though how I cannot tell. They must have gone there for shelter and it seemed as if the Lord had shut them in. As I stood at the cowyard gate leading into the field I was almost frightened at the fury of the wind, the blasts were so awful that I feared one of the great elms must fall. Sometimes the tempest rose to such a furious and ungovernable pitch as if hell had been let loose, that it seemed as if something must go, and as if the very world itself must give way and be shattered to atoms. The very beasts seemed frightened and the dog lay close in his kennel and would not come out. I went round to the front of the house and stood on the stone steps and wondered at the wind and thought of the poor people on Clyro Hill and prayed for those at sea. 'For at his word the stormy wind ariseth which lifteth up the waves thereof.' The whole world seemed to be groaning and straining under the press of that dreadful wind. All the evening the wind roared and thundered and the tempest grew wilder and more wild, and if damage was done we could not hear it. Everything was drowned in the roar and thunder of the storm. The wind howled down the chimney, the room was full of smoke and every now and then the fire flaught out into the room in tongues of flame beaten down with a smother of sparks and smoke.

MONDAY, 16 DECEMBER

Dame Matthews used to live at the Home Farm at Langley Burrell. She was a member of the family, but she must have lived a long time ago, as Mrs Banks remarked, because she called cows 'kine'. The Dame used to sit in the chimney corner and near her chair there was a little window through which she could see all down the dairy. One evening she saw one of the farm men steal a pound of butter out of the dairy and put it into his hat, at the same moment clapping his hat upon his head.

'John,' called the Dame. 'John, come here. I want to speak to you.' John came, carefully keeping his hat on his head. The Dame ordered some ale to be heated for him and bade him sit down in front of the roaring fire. John thanked his mistress and said he would have the ale another time, as he wanted to go home at once.

'No, John. Sit you down by the fire and drink some hot ale. 'Tis a cold night and I want to speak to you about the kine.'

The miserable John, daring neither to take off his hat nor go without his mistress's leave, sat before the scorching fire drinking his hot ale till the melting butter in his hat began to run down all over his face. The Dame eyed him with malicious fun. 'Now, John,' she said, 'you may go. I won't charge you anything for the butter.'

TUESDAY, NEW YEAR'S EVE

My Mother says the old Langley people always used to say that the Langley Burrell bells rang these words, 'My cow's tail's long, my cow's tail's long.'

— 1873 —

TUESDAY, 7 JANUARY

At 8 o'clock Fanny, Dora and I went to a jolly party at Sir John Awdry's at Norton House. Almost everybody in the neighbourhood was there. There had been a children's party with a Christmas Tree at 5 o'clock, but when we drove up the harp and the fiddles were going.

I danced a Lancers with Harriet Awdry of Draycot Rectory, a quadrille with Sissy Awdry of Seagry Vicarage, a Lancers with Louise Awdry of Draycot Rectory, a Lancers with Mary Rooke of the Ivy, and Sir Roger with dear little Francie Rooke of the Ivy. How bright and pretty she looked, so merry, happy and full of fun. It was a grand Sir Roger. I never danced such a one. The room was quite full, two sets and such long lines, but the crush was all the more fun. 'Here,' said Francie Rooke to me quietly, with a wild, merrie sparkle in her eye, and her face brilliant with excitement, 'let us go into the other set.' There was more fun going on there, Eliza Stiles had just fallen prostrate. There were screams of laughter and the dance was growing quite wild. There was a struggle for the corners and everyone wanted to be at the top. In a few minutes all order was lost, and everyone was dancing wildly and promiscuously with whoever came to hand. The dance grew wilder and wilder. 'The pipers loud and louder blew, the dancers quick and quicker flew.' Madder and madder screamed the flying fiddle bows. Sir Roger became a wild romp till the fiddles suddenly stopped dead and there was a scream of laughter. Oh, it was such fun and Francie Rooke was brilliant. When shall I have another such partner as Francie Rooke?

An excellent supper and we got home about one o'clock, on a fine moonlit night.

THURSDAY, 9 JANUARY

The earthly troubles of the exiled Emperor are over. At eleven o'clock this morning Napoleon III passed away at Camden House, Chislehurst. He died very suddenly and quietly. He had undergone several severe operations by Sir Henry Thompson for crushing the stone in the bladder. Another operation, the last, was contemplated, and the symptoms and condition of the patient were all favourable when suddenly at 10 o'clock this morning to the surprise of the doctors the pulse fluttered and in a few minutes Napoleon breathed his last quietly and without pain. It is supposed that a clot of blood rose to the heart and suffocated him.

It has been a life of marvellous vicissitudes and the most wonderful romance since that of Charles Edward.

SATURDAY, 11 JANUARY

Dora went to Langley House and found poor Syddy Ashe in agonies of grief at the Emperor's death.

SUNDAY, 12 JANUARY

When I came out the night was superb. The sky was cloudless, the moon rode high and full in the deep blue vault and the evening star blazed in the west. The air was filled with the tolling and chiming of bells from St Paul's and Chippenham old Church. The night was soft and still and I walked up and down the drive several times before I could make up my mind to leave the wonderful beauty of the night and go indoors. To be alone out of doors on a still soft clear moonlit night is to me one of the greatest pleasures that this world can give.

THURSDAY, 23 JANUARY

After I had been at the school I went at ten o'clock to Langley House to beard the lion in his den. I found Mr and Mrs Ashe in the dining room. She had just finished reading *The Times* to him. I plunged at once *in medias res*. He said that he wished the money could be procured in the old-fashioned way by the ancient machinery of Church rate, and so much the worse for those who refused to pay. The Squire begged that the Church should not be washed with yellow ochre. I got his consent to the Communion Service being read from the altar, and Mrs Ashe backed me up staunchly and proposed that two chairs should be got to stand within the rails. The Squire seemed rather surprised at the idea of a clergyman sitting within the rails during the service and thought that he should not 'lounge' in a chair.

FRIDAY, FEBRUARY EVE

When I came home last night at half past twelve I was surprised by seeing lights still burning in the house and Dora let me in. I never saw my dear sister look so pretty. A black cloak was thrown round her and her bright hair fell like a cloud over her shoulders. She had been playing chess with my Father. The fire was still burning in the dining room. We stood a few minutes to warm ourselves. Then a shower of sweet kisses and I sent the dear pretty girl to bed.

TUESDAY, 4 FEBRUARY

Sat an hour with John and Hannah Hatherell at tea. I read to them and they told me the story of the terrible faction fight between the men at Chippenham and the men of the two Langleys years ago, in which two Chippenham men were killed. Hall the saddler and Reynolds the tinman. The quarrel between Chippenham and the Langleys had been long brewing and there was bad blood and a bitter feud between the town and the two villages. It was the fault of Chippenham. They began it. A lot of Chippenham blackguards had been in the habit of ill-using and beating the Langley men whenever the country folk came into the town on the market day which was then Saturday. Things came to such a pass that the Langley people could not enter the town without being abused and knocked about and they were afraid to go to market. This state of things was not to be borne and the men of Langley Fitzurse arranged to go into Chippenham in force on a certain market day and avenge their insults and injuries. A number of Langley Burrell men joined them and the united force armed with sticks and bludgeons and numbering perhaps from 30 to 40 men entered the town on a market day, Saturday afternoon. Some folk say it was a cunning plot and that the whole scheme was preconcerted, but at all events what happened was this. After some fierce fighting in the streets with fists, sticks and stones, after many heads had been broken and some blood had been spilt the Langley men retreated up the hill in a body as far as the Little George where a turnpike then stood. Here they stood. The Chippenham men taunted and reviled them and called to come on like men and not to run home like women. The Langley men having gained their purpose and having drawn their enemies out of the town now turned fiercely and charged upon them down the hill. The stones flew like hail. Strong men were beaten down. Eyes were knocked out and the road ran with blood. The Chippenham blackguards were driven back pell-mell in wild confusion into the town, the 30 or 40 Langley men driving a mob of 200 before them like sheep. The scene in the streets was fearful. One of the Chippenham blackguards had his eye knocked out with a stone. But unhappily innocent men suffered with the guilty. Hull the saddler and Reynolds the tinman came out to quell the riot. They got into the mob and were irresistibly and helplessly borne away by the crowd down the Bath road by the Ivy, in which direction the fight was surging. They were never able to regain their houses and were both killed. Hull was set up dead upon the 'turn train' (turnstile) going to Beck Avon Bridge between Chippenham and the Ivy where the posts stand now. A Langley man found Reynolds lying on the ground with his head almost beaten to pieces and raised the poor fellow's head on his knee, but the hair and skin and flesh came off in flakes when it was touched. Reynolds only spoke one word. 'Mountjoy,' he muttered. Mountjoy was a Langley man and it was always supposed that he gave the fatal blow but no one knows.

Jerry Knight, the carpenter at the top of Huntsman's Hill, was Constable and Mr Sheppard of the Brewery was 'Tyddyman' of the parish. On this Saturday night John Hatherell had been brewing for Mr Sheppard and on Sunday morning as he was at the Brewery he suddenly saw the courtyard filled with people from Chippenham and the constables were going about among the cottages making arrests of the Langley men who were suspected of having been engaged in the riot overnight. Old John Thomas the carpenter, then a lusty young man, ran down to John Hatherell's cottage and leaned up against the dresser as white as a sheet. Hannah asked him if he had been in the fight. 'No,' he said. But he had, and he was arrested, tried, and sent to jail. Farmer Matthews of Rawlings and Henry Knight were both in the riot and had to go to jail.

The prisoners were kept at a public house in Chippenham waiting their turn for examination and trial and
Hannah Hatherell looked through the window and saw
them all chained to a long iron bar.

Scarcely any of the Chippenham men were arrested
and examined. Most of the blackguards got off scot-free.
And this was most unjust because they began the quarrel
and the Langley men would never come into Chippenham to fight unless they had been terribly provoked.
The poor Langley fellows too were beaten black and
blue and fearfully knocked about.

John Hatherell said that old Langley Common was
once a great play place on Sunday, and on Sunday afternoons football and hockey and other games went on all
over the common. The Revd Samuel Ashe, then Rector
of Langley Burrell, used to come round quietly under
the trees and bide his time till the football came near
him when he would catch up the ball and pierce the
bladder with a pin. But some of the young fellows would
be even with the parson for they would bring a spare
bladder, blow it, and soon have the football flying again.

FRIDAY, 7 FEBRUARY

Coal still rising. £2.11. a ton in London now. We are
burning coke with wood and find it answers very well.
The poor people are very badly off for coal. The coal
famine is becoming most serious. And the colliers' strike
in South Wales seems to have entered upon a desperately
bitter and obstinate struggle with the masters, a struggle
to be fought out now to the death and till one party or

the other is utterly exhausted. Meanwhile innocent men, non-unionists, and women and children are dying of cold and hunger.

MONDAY, 10 FEBRUARY

My Mother says that at Dursley in Gloucestershire, when ladies and gentlemen used to go out to dinner together on dark nights, the gentlemen pulled out the tails of their shirts and walked before to show the way and light the ladies. These were called 'Dursley Lanterns'.

TUESDAY, 11 FEBRUARY

A letter from Mr Venables from Clyro asking me if my Father could spare me to come to Clyro and take charge of the Parish from March 3rd to March 22nd as Irvine leaves at the end of February and he himself wants to be in London during part of March. I wrote immediately to say 'yes'. How pleasant it will be seeing the dear old place and people again.

ASH WEDNESDAY, 26 FEBRUARY

My dear Father's birthday. My Father read the Commination from the pulpit.

FRIDAY, MARCH EVE

I went to Hardenhuish House. Between St Paul's Church and the Lodge an old man stood by the way-side begging.

He was quite blind, and beside him stood a pretty girl, his granddaughter, with curling chestnut hair and beautiful roguish merry eyes. She had gathered some primroses and stuck them in her brown straw hat. And when I came up the child pretended to be shy, got behind her grandfather and seemed to be looking along the bank for more flowers. I stopped and spoke to the old man. 'I am fourscore,' he said. 'For sixty years I worked at the blast furnaces and the fire was too strong for my eyes. I came out here to stand and try if I could gather a few coppers as it is market day.'

MONDAY, 3 MARCH

Returned to Clyro to take charge of the parish for three weeks, two Sundays for Mr Venables.

Reached Hay at 1.18 and going to the Castle joined the Bevans at luncheon. As I walked over to Clyro I overtook Mrs Williams of Little Wern y Pentre hobbling home with her stick, and Hannah. She was almost overcome and besought me to stay with them and never to leave them again. 'You know what we want,' she said. 'We want you to live at the Vicarage.' Alas, it is not in my power. At the school the dear children were on the look out for me. Afternoon school was just over and they were clustering in the playground and some walking along the road towards the Hay – such exclamations of delight and smiles of loving welcome and faces lighted up and flushed with pleasure. It was very touching to be so welcomed back. Mrs Rogers (Pring) makes me most comfortable at the Vicarage and quite spoils me.

TUESDAY, 4 MARCH

I have the bedroom at the Vicarage looking towards the south and the mountains. How sweet once more to see the morning spread upon the mountains.

Mrs Chaloner says I must put myself in a cage to-day or the old women will tear me to pieces for joy. I have been villaging all day. The welcome of the people is very touching.

There are changes in Clyro since I left. Six or seven of the old familiar faces have passed away in those six months. Dear little Lily Crichton, aged 7 years, and the patriarch William Williams of Crowther's Pool, aged fourscore years and ten, William Price of the Stocks House, aged 85 years, and sweet Margaret Gore of Whitty's Mill in the bloom of her youth and 20 years. Edward Evans has left us, having just fulfilled his three-score and ten. The troubles of poor mad Margaret Meredith (entered in the Burial Register of the Parish as Margaret Mulready) have ended in her 62nd year. And the sufferings of John Powell the blacksmith closed when he wanted but two years to complete the 'day of our age'.

There are changes too in the landscape of Clyro for the trees have all been felled on the Castle mound which now looks bare and dreary.

WEDNESDAY, 5 MARCH

After Church I went to see Hannah Whitney and she received the Holy Communion for the first time at the age of fourscore years and ten.

FRIDAY, 7 MARCH

In the afternoon I drove to Whitney Rectory in the dog-cart to dine and sleep. An April day and showers and shine with exquisitely clear views of the mountains and two beautiful rainbows. Before dinner Emily, Jane and Armine Dew walked with me up through the steep hanging wood above the railway, carpeted with prim-roses upbreaking through the earth. After dinner Henry Dew told us some of his old hunting reminiscences of the days when he rode with the Maesllwch fox-hounds.

Charles Lacy was out with the Radnorshire and West Herefordshire fox-hounds when they met at Cabalva last Wednesday. He gave an amusing description of the run. Old Tom Evans, the tailor, of Cwm Ithel on Clyro Hill, was once a running huntsman with the Clyro har-riers, and very keen after the sport. When he heard the hunting horns along the hill on Wednesday the old hunting instinct in him awoke like a giant refreshed. He scrambled on to his old pony and rode furiously into the middle of the pack hat in hand hooping and holloing and laying the hounds on to the scent as of yore. Colonel Price the M.F.H. was greatly enraged. 'Man! Man!' he shouted. 'Where are you going, man? Come from those hounds!' But the tailor maddened with the chase was deaf to all entreaties and commands. He careered along among and over the hounds, hooping, holloing and waving his hat till the enraged M.F.H. charged him and knocked tailor and pony head over heels. Nothing daunted however the tailor scrambled on to his beast again and he and his pony were second in at the death, close at the heels of the M.F.H.

Charles Lacy said the bag fox had been kept in a dark cellar so long that he was dazed and half blind when he was turned out. After they had killed the bag fox they tried for a wild one at Dolbedwyn, where some poultry had been stolen by a fox.

SATURDAY, 8 MARCH

At eleven o'clock the dog-cart came for me with the chestnut old Rocket, and I returned to Clyro.

Amelia Meredith tells me that at Llanhollantine people used to go to the church door at midnight to hear the saints within call over the names of those who were to die within the year. Also they heard the sound of the pew doors opening and shutting though no one was in the church.

SATURDAY, 15 MARCH

I caught a chill yesterday in the snow at Emmeline's grave and tossed all night in a fever.

I had heard that William Meredith of the Tump just above Whitty's Mill was very sick, and going to the house I found him dying. As I sat talking with the dying man and as we knelt round the bed the tempest shook the old house and roared in the roof so as almost to drown my voice, and the dying man rolled his eyes wildly in the darkness of the curtained bed.

A bitter east wind blew furiously over the hills as I stood at the exposed door of Llwyn Gwillim.

At the lone cottage in the Chapel Dingle my dear friend sweet Emma Griffiths was almost beside herself with delight when I opened the door. But her joy was soon turned into sorrow. I had not many minutes to stay and when I rose to go poor Emma clasped my hands in both of hers, gave me a long loving look and turned away with a burst of weeping, in a passion of tears. What is it? What is it? What do they all mean? It is a strange and terrible gift, this power of stealing hearts and exciting such love.

At the new Chapel Farm I found Wall and his wife at home and little Nellie lay lovingly in my arms.

I ran down to Cabalva and called at Whitcombe's at the Bronith. Saw Mrs Watkeys and kissed her two beautiful grandchildren as the girls sat together by the fire.

Found Mrs Potts the keeper's wife among the tubs surrounded by naked girls and boys whom she was washing and putting to bed. Spent a quarter of an hour, my last, with the old soldier John Morgan and his wife Mary, and reached home just in time for dinner at Cae Mawr with the Morrells, almost worn out with running, talking, and different emotions. I had been obliged to run almost all the way between the various houses.

SUNDAY, 16 MARCH

The bitter cold east wind yesterday ended in a heavy fall of snow this morning about 4 inches on the level of the Vicarage lawn. Scarcely any people were at Church at either service.

The madness, cloud and delirium I trust has passed away at length. 'And it came to pass that when the devil was gone out the dumb spake.' I can write again now.

TUESDAY, 18 MARCH

Old James Jones the sawyer of the Infant School told me that he remembers a reprobate drunken fellow named James Davies, but nicknamed 'Jim of the Dingle' being put in the stocks at Clyro by Archdeacon Venables and the parish constable. This Jim of the Dingle had a companion spirit as wicked as himself. And both of them belonged to the Herefordshire Militia. So when the Archdeacon and the Constable had gone away leaving Jim in the stocks, Jim's friend brought an axe and beat the stocks all to pieces and let the prisoner out. The two worthies fled away to Hereford to the militia and never returned to Clyro. But the Clyro people, seeing the stocks broken, demolished and burnt the stocks and the whipping post, and no one was ever confined or whipped at Clyro after that.

WEDNESDAY, 19 MARCH

I drove to Llan Thomas to dine and sleep. Daisy was very good to me all the evening. She taught me to play Commerce, and thinking the lamp hurt my eyes as I shaded them a moment with the cards to look across the table she rose at once and brought the lampshade. She asked anxiously if my cough hurt me and whenever I coughed she seemed to suffer pain herself.

[The diarist returns to Langley Burrell.]

WEDNESDAY, 9 APRIL

While we were sitting at supper this evening we were startled by a sound under the sideboard as if a rat were tearing and gnawing at the wainscot or skirting board. The noise ceased and then began again. Suddenly Dora uttered an exclamation and a strange look came over her face. She seized the lamp and went to the sideboard pointing to a white-handled knife which lay under the sideboard and which she said she had seen a moment before crawling and wriggling along the floor-cloth by itself and making the tearing, gnawing, rending noise we had heard. No one knew how the knife had got under the sideboard. As four of us stood round looking at the knife lying on the floorcloth suddenly the knife leaped into the air and fell back without anyone touching it. It looked very strange and startled us a good deal. We thought of spirit agency and felt uncomfortable and compared the time expecting to hear more of the matter, until Dora observed a very tiny grey mouse taking the buttered point of the knife in his mouth and dragging it along and walking backwards. Then all was explained.

FRIDAY, 18 APRIL

My mother says she remembers to have heard as an old village tradition that the street of Kington St Michael was green with grass during the Great Plague for there was scarcely any passing in those dreadful months.

MONDAY, 19 MAY

Went to London by 11.15 train. At half past four I met Jack in the vestibule at Burlington House. The Exhibition seemed to me to be an unusually good one, and I was much struck by some of the pictures especially sweet Imogen, and the Turning Point, the beautiful face and eyes of the wife looking up to her husband's stern sullen countenance as she leans on his breast, beseeching him, pleading with him, oh so earnestly and imploringly, to give up drinking. It went to my heart.

HOLY THURSDAY, 22 MAY

I went to the International Exhibition and saw the silk looms weaving and bought some medals of the Queen, Prince of Wales and the Exhibition which I saw being struck. One of the most beautiful pictures was one of a lovely girl reaper. At 5 o'clock I went into the Park. At Hyde Park Corner the crush was incredible.

FRIDAY, 23 MAY

How delighted to get down into the sweet fresh damp air of the country again and the scent of the bean blossoms.

WEDNESDAY, 11 JUNE

Drove my Mother to Kington St Michael in a shandry dan which was lent to us by Hart Porter while he is repainting and repairing our own carriage. In Gander Lane we saw in the banks some of the 'Midsummer Men' plants which my Mother remembers the servant maids and cottage girls sticking up in their houses and bedrooms on Midsummer Eve, for the purpose of divining about their sweethearts.

SUNDAY, 15 JUNE

A beautiful peaceful summer Sunday morn such as Robert Burns would have loved. Perfect peace and rest. The sun and the golden buttercup meadows had it almost all to themselves. A few soft fleecy clouds were rising out of the west but the gentle warm air scarcely stirred even the leaves on the lofty tops of the great poplars. One or two people were crossing the Common early by the several paths through the golden sea of buttercups which will soon be the silver sea of ox-eyes. The birds were singing quietly. The cuckoo's notes tolled clear and sweet as a silver bell and a dove was pleading in the elm and 'making intercession for us with groanings which cannot be uttered'.

WEDNESDAY, 18 JUNE

This evening the Shah of Persia arrived in England from Brussels and Ostend, escorted by the British fleet, and got wetted through by a heavy shower as he drove from the Railway Station to Buckingham Palace. The Shah is the first Persian monarch who ever left his own dominions except for conquest.

SATURDAY, 12 JULY

This afternoon I went to see Mrs Drew and if possible to comfort her concerning the death of her child. She was filled with sorrow and remorse because when the child had mouched from school last Monday and had wandered about all day with scarcely any food she had whipped him as soon as he came home in the evening and had sent him supperless to bed, although he had besought her almost in an agony to give him a bit of bread. 'Oh Mother, oh Mother, do give me one bit of bread.' Her heart smote her bitterly now that it was too late, when she remembered how the child had begged and prayed for food. The next morning soon after rising he fell down in a fit and he died at seven. The mother asked me to go upstairs and see the child. He lay in his coffin looking very peaceful and natural with the flowers on his breast and the dark hair curling on his forehead.

WEDNESDAY, 16 JULY

As I walked along the field path I stopped to listen to the rustle and solemn night whisper of the wheat, so different to its voice by day. The corn seemed to be praising God and whispering its evening prayer. Across the great level meads near Chippenham came the martial music of a drum and fife band, and laughing voices of unseen girls were wafted from farms and hayfields out of the wide dusk.

MONDAY, 21 JULY

A splendid summer's day, burning hot, sitting under the linden reading *Memorials of a Quiet Life*, Augustus Hare's book. As I sat there my mind went through a fierce struggle. Right or wrong? The right conquered, the sin was repented and put away and the rustle of the wind and the melodious murmurs of innumerable bees in the hives overhead suddenly seemed to me to take the sound of distant music, organs. And I thought I heard the harps of the angels rejoicing in heaven over a sinner that had repented. Then I thought I saw an angel in an azure robe coming towards me across the lawn, but it was only the blue sky through the feathering branches of the lime.

TUESDAY, 22 JULY

To-day the heat was excessive and as I sat reading under the lime I pitied the poor haymakers toiling in the burning Common where it seemed to be raining fire.

WEDNESDAY, 23 JULY

Came to Hawkchurch for three days. A pleasant and lovely journey with the air cleared and cooled by the storm. Uncle Will met me at Axminster Station with Polly and the dog cart.

After tea Dora and I went up the high field in front of the cottage to look for mushrooms and glow worms in the dusk.

THURSDAY, 24 JULY

This morning Uncle Will, Dora and I drove to Seaton with Polly and the dog cart. It was a lovely morning. At Seaton while Dora was sitting on the beach I had a bathe. A boy brought me to the machine door two towels as I thought, but when I came out of the water and began to use them I found that one of the rags he had given me was a pair of very short red and white striped drawers to cover my nakedness. Unaccustomed to such things and customs I had in my ignorance bathed naked and set at nought the conventionalities of the place and scandalized the beach. However some little boys who were looking on at the rude naked man appeared to be much interested in the spectacle, and the young ladies who were strolling near seemed to have no objection.

SATURDAY, 26 JULY

Up at 6.30 and out at 7 o'clock in a lovely bright breezy morning, the dew shining after rain. I stole out at the back door to avoid disturbing anyone and I believe Rawlings the gardener thought I was gone mad or going to commit suicide for he ran anxiously out of his shoe house and looked after me to see which way I was going. The meadows were clean swept and washed and the lattermath from which the hay had been cleared gleamed brilliant green after the rain. I followed the lanes past West Hay, and presently came to the dry bed of a brook crossing the road. Before I could pass over it however I heard a sudden sound of water and saw a stream beginning to trickle and wind amongst the stones. The stream broadened and deepened till with a swift rush of brown turbid water the brook bed was filled and the stream poured under a little foot bridge and roared down, a small cataract, into the meadows beyond. I thought at first it was a little flood caused by the day and night's rain and just came down the valley, but a merry-faced peasant, who was on his way to a rustic festival of sheep dipping, said that the sudden stream I had seen was the water fresh loosed from the mill pound of Zealey's Mill at Phelley Holme. The man said there were a good many trout in the brooks from ½ lb. to 2 lbs. and told me they should probably end their sheep dipping with a trout-netting frolic in the evening after the work was done.

At the bottom of the hill in the sunny hollow where we crossed a little stream of limpid water clear as crystal, dazzling and gleaming over its yellow pebbles, we met a woman who in answer to my companion's enquiries directed him to the sheepwashing. And presently we came to the gate of the meadow where the rural festival was being held. A group of men whose clothes were splashed and dyed by the red wash were plunging sheep and lambs one by one into a long deep trough. The sheep went in white and came out red, protected by their dipping against the attentions of the fly, and walked away across the meadow to join the flock, shaking the red wash in showers from their close-shorn fleeces.

The lane grew more and still more lovely. The morning sunlight slanted richly across the road between the trees, or struck here and there through a break in the foliage and tipped a frond of fern with brilliant green light. Broad alternate bars of sunshine and shadow lay across the lane, the sunlight shone on the polished grey silvery stems of a row of beeches, and a tender morning mist hung dreamily over the wooded hollow of the dingle below the road.

The lane opened up into a high open common across which the morning breeze from the sea stirred freshly with a cool light after the warm shelter of the hollow lanes. Beyond the common a gate let into a shady road cool and damp, dark and quiet as a cloister. It was completely overhung by trees, and the air was filled with the fragrant aromatic scent of the fir trees and the soft carpet of fir needles with which the ground was thickly strewn. The fields of ripening wheat began to glow golden along the slopes of the blue hills and the ferns, fresh washed by the rain of the night, beamed clear and brilliant green where the sun slanted silently through the windows of the wood.

TUESDAY, 19 AUGUST

Went to see Mrs Pearce at Landsend, Mrs James Knight's sister. She told me her sad story. Born in better circumstances, the daughter of a substantial but litigious farmer, her mother died while she was yet a child. Then her husband died young leaving her with two children and a farm at Shaw to struggle with. Her cows caught the distemper and she was forced to drench them with her own hands. Next the rent of her farm was suddenly and greatly raised by her own brother-in-law and she was in consequence thrown out of business and reduced to comparative poverty. 'Twas a sad history and when she had asked me about my own family and had learnt that my Father and Mother were both living, she said with a sigh, 'How different some people's circumstances are'. 'I used,' she said, 'to look across the road to the churchyard where my husband was sleeping and think how he was lying at rest while I had all the cares of the farm and the family to struggle with. And I thought my heart would break.'

SATURDAY, 30 AUGUST

Driving into Chippenham with Fanny this morning we saw the headquarters of the 13th Hussars who had just marched in, band playing. They were on their way up from Dartmoor to Colchester. They had been taking part in the disastrous manoeuvres. Horses and men looked thin, worn, weak, dirty and jaded and as if the best manoeuvres they could accomplish would be a manoeuvre into their barracks. They have had a sad time on Dartmoor, incessant rain and bottomless swamp and no rugs for the horses who stood fetlock deep in the bogs. Capt. Dallin was in the town, delighted to see soldiers again and quite in his element. There was a good deal of excitement and movement in the town. Officers riding about billeting the men and men seeking their billets.

TUESDAY, SEPTEMBER MORROW

In the evening Dora went to Langley Lodge to see Mrs Dallin and as she did not come back by dark I went to fetch her. A soft moonlight was flooding the common as the moon sailed out from behind a net of heavy clouds and the cattle looked ghostly in the weird silver light. At Langley Lodge I found two dashing Hussars dining with Captain Dallin who was in his glory. Captain Truman and a subaltern in his troop, Lieutenant Burne I think. The Lieutenant found his dress Hussar boot very tight at dessert and in great agony he begged my pen knife. Then while I held a candle from the branches he by Captain Truman's advice slit his boot up the side and found immediate relief, though with some compunction for the boots were his best and last pair.

WEDNESDAY, 3 SEPTEMBER

This morning punctually at 7.30 the bugle sounded the trot at the top of Huntsman's Hill and the last troop of the 13th Hussars clanked along the Common. Captain

Truman was as good as his word. They took the road down the village and stopped at Langley Lodge where Captain Dallin regaled the officers with brandy and soda. One morning before he gave them brandy and soda on the Common.

FRIDAY, 19 SEPTEMBER

At Rawling's I was talking to old Mrs Matthews about the great number of railway accidents that have happened lately. 'It's shocking to be ushered out of the world in that way,' exclaimed Alice Matthews indignantly. John Couzens foretells a revolution in English society. 'I know it's coming,' he said, 'as sure as this prong is in my hand.'

WEDNESDAY, 24 SEPTEMBER

Another glorious day added to this beautiful Michael-mas summer. As I walked before breakfast across the Common I met Herriman the porter returning through the lovely morning from his night work at the station, and I could not help thinking of the difference between my lot and his, and how much more enjoyment I have in my life than he has in his. How differently we both spent last night, but how much better he spent it than I did. He was doing extra night duty that a fellow porter might enjoy a holiday, while I . . . Herriman has only three days' holiday during the whole year, while to me every day is a holiday and enjoyment and delight. And for no desert of mine. Surely there will be compensation made for these things hereafter if not here.

SUNDAY, MICHAELMAS EVE

Dora said Syddy Ashe is fairly mad with disappointment at not having seen the 13th Hussars when they passed through Langley on their way to Colchester. 'I would have given a great deal to have seen one,' she said, 'it would have been happiness to have seen one soldier, but to have missed the chance of seeing them all! It is too much.' And she nearly cried with vexation.

TUESDAY, 7 OCTOBER

This morning I went to Bath with my Father and Mother to attend the Church Congress Service at the Abbey at 11. Dr Alexander the Bishop of Derry preached an admirable sermon nearly an hour long.

The swarming city was filled with the ringing of bells. At 2 my Mother, Thersie and I went to a meeting in the new temporary Congress Hall, where we heard more good papers and speeches from the Bishop of Bath and Wells, the President of the Congress, the Bishop of Oxford, Lord Bath, Lord Nelson, Beresford Hope, and Canon Girdlestone on 'the duty of the Church with regard to strikes and labour'.

WEDNESDAY, 8 OCTOBER

This morning I came down to Bath from Chippenham to stay for the rest of the Congress. I reached Bath just in time to go up to the new wooden Congress Hall, admirably arranged for sound and ventilation, and attended two sections, the first on Foreign Missions and the second on the Union of Church and State. In the first section Sir Bartle Frere spoke admirably. Last night and this afternoon George Anthony Denison spoke and excited a storm.

THURSDAY, 9 OCTOBER

Lunched at 1 Sion Hill with Miss Armine Furlong, Miss Reece and Jane Drew and went to three sections of the Church Congress.

FRIDAY, 10 OCTOBER

Attended three sections of the Church Congress at the Congress Hall. The subjects were the Life of Godliness, the Religious wants and claims of children, and Church Music. In the morning, as Bishop Ryan was speaking, an angel came into the Congress Hall and stood near the door listening. It had taken the form of a very beautiful young girl in a long grey cloak and a shower of golden-brown hair. I watched her intently and as she bowed her fair head and knee at the Name of Names she assumed exactly the attitude and appearance of the angels that overshadowed with their wings the ark and the Mercy seat. In the perpetual struggle between the powers and principles of good and evil the obeisance rebuked and put to flight an evil thought.

After the last section on Church Music I went with Miss Armine Furlong, Miss Reece and Jane Dew to the Mayor and Mayoress's reception at the Assembly Rooms.

Some 3000 people were present and yet there was plenty of space to walk about in these noble rooms. We arrived at 9 and left at midnight. There was a band, tea, coffee, ices, champagne cup, claret cup, sandwiches, and speeches by the Bishop of Peterborough, the Bishop of Manchester, the Rector of Bath, and Mr Randall, Vicar of All Saints, Clifton.

It was stated that the Bath Congress was the most successful and the largest Church Congress yet held, 1400 more tickets having been sold than last year at Leeds. Altogether between 6000 and 7000 tickets were sold.

WEDNESDAY, 22 OCTOBER

This evening I had a letter from Josiah Evans, my friend the Clyro schoolmaster. His letter makes me laugh and almost cry at the same time. The parish he says is all in a muddle from end to end, and the sooner the new Vicar comes the better. My poor Clyro. My beloved Clyro.

WEDNESDAY, 29 OCTOBER

Dined at Chippenham Vicarage with Fanny. The Jacksons were there, Georgie and George Awdry with Miss Lucy Peck and the Frederick Awdrys with Capt. Hill, their cousin, a tall handsome powerful man who when tiger hunting once in India was seized by a tiger by the back of his neck. But he so pommelled the tiger's face over his shoulder that the beast let go, leaving Capt. Hill however with a stiff neck for life.

MONDAY, 17 NOVEMBER

At ten o'clock this morning, after school, I went on to
Langley House to consult Mr Ashe about the advisability
of publicly observing the Special Day of Prayer for
Missionaries which the Archbishop of Canterbury has
recommended for December 3. I found the Squire and
Mrs Ashe in the upper drawing room. She was reading
aloud to him. He asked whether I thought it wise to
have lectures on winter evenings for mixed audiences of
men and women, and to bring out the girls and their
sweethearts for a moonlight walk.

THURSDAY, 20 NOVEMBER

Edward Humphries married a young woman when he
was 83 and had a son within the year. 'Leastways his
wife had,' said Mrs Hall.

FRIDAY, 28 NOVEMBER

Dined at Langley House. Only the Dallins were there.
The Squire was very agreeable, and gave us some of
his splendid old '51 port and some priceless Madeira
thirty-five years old, imported when Emma Clutterbuck
was at Madeira.

SUNDAY, 7 DECEMBER

Called on old Sally Killing after Church. She asked me
the usual and indeed invariable question whether I

remembered her old thatched cottage, near the road, by the lilac bush, and the old house in Westfield. I asked her how she passed her time. 'Aw ther,' she said, 'I do rock and sway myself about.'

TUESDAY, 9 DECEMBER

A brilliant white frost and the hoary meadows sparkling with millions of rainbows and twinkling with diamonds.

From the gate of Langley House, while waiting for Dora and Georgie to come out, I saw the Squire in his white hat cantering his bay pony across the park and charging the phalanx of his daughters on the gravel in front of the house to see how they would 'resist cavalry', his usual joke. The infantry scattered right and left and Thersie flew off to a safe distance.

Mrs Coates told me of her son Reuben's noble conduct to his dying sweetheart Sarah Hains. He would not be ashamed of her nor cease walking with her though her dropsical size drew all eyes and many suspicions upon him.

WEDNESDAY, 10 DECEMBER

Sad accounts reach me of the neglected state of my poor Clyro. 'My sheep wander through the mountains.'

FRIDAY, 12 DECEMBER

Walked with Dora to Langley Fitzurse. Called at the Manor Farm and had a long chat with Alice Banks about old times.

When Miss Long became heiress of Draycot and Wanstead and came of age there were great rejoicings. An ox was roasted whole in the park and a troop of yeomanry cavalry guarded it, riding round the roasting ox to keep the people off. When the ox was cut down half of it was burnt and charred and the other half was raw.

Thousands of people gathered from far and near to see the rejoicing. While the cavalry were at dinner in the house the kitchen chimney caught fire. The cavalry rushed out to see what was the matter, and the crowd immediately rushed in and cleared the tables. There was no food to be got in Sutton, all the provisions were swept off. Many of the strangers were nearly starved and came to the Home farm, where Mrs Banks was visiting her grandfather, to ask for some dry bread and cold water for which they were ready to pay anything. But the house was nearly empty of food. There was a ball in the great barn too and horse racing in the Park with all sorts of games and fireworks in the evening.

Then came the courtship and marriage of Miss Long, the great heiress, with the scamp Wellesley. Lady Catherine set her face against the marriage, but her daughter was weak and obstinate, the servants were bribed and the courtship was carried on clandestinely. Wellesley used to drive his tilbury down to the Langley Brewery, leave it there, and come and hide himself in the sunk fence in front of this house, what is now Langley Rectory. When he had watched Lady Catherine drive across the common into Chippenham with her four or six long-tailed black horses, leaving Miss Long the heiress locked up at home, he would run down to the Brewery, get into his tilbury, and gallop over to Draycot, where he saw Miss Long by the connivance of the servants.

She was infatuated and would not listen to those friends who told her that he was a villain and only wanted her money. Afterwards he brought down a hired carriage and horses from London and drove from the Angel at Chippenham to Draycot four-in-hand. At length Lady Catherine gave way and consented to the marriage, which Miss Long never ceased to regret, for her husband treated her in the most brutal manner and squandered the estate.

Mrs Banks said that one night her father came home from Chippenham very much disgusted because Long Wellesley had said in an election speech when he was standing for the county, 'Now gentlemen, all of you who are husbands, I advise you to go home and be as good husbands to your wives as I am to mine.' The impudent scoundrel.

Isaac Giles says he remembers hearing Long Wellesley make an election speech from the Angel in the course of which he told the people how he had 'got up the old lady's legs and married her daughter'. Isaac Giles was then working next door to the Angel and saw Long Wellesley drive away to Draycot four-in-hand every morning courting, and return at night. As he left Church with his bride after the wedding he was tapped on the shoulder for £20,000. And my mother remembers the wretched wife not long afterwards coming up to Langley Fitzurse, to my grandfather's, to borrow money, for the bailiffs were in Draycot House and her scamp of a husband had left her destitute. She was a mean-looking little woman, as weak as water.

MONDAY, 15 DECEMBER

Fanny went to luncheon at Langley Fitzurse. I called there at 1.30 and walked to Draycot with her to see Draycot House. Miss West the housekeeper showed us over the house. The entrance hall was matted with fallow deer skins from the chase. The walls were ornamented with fallow bucks' heads and horns from every branch tip of which sprung a jet of gas.

To-day Captain Wellesley was married to the daughter of Lord Augustus Loftus. The bride and bridegroom were expected down by the 5 o'clock train to spend the honeymoon at Draycot. About an hour and a half before they arrived we were being shown through their bedroom, dressing and sitting rooms and looking at their photographs. Coming home I met Mrs Ashe and as I stood talking to her in the dusk, there came a flashing of lights and a rattle of horse-hoofs and the bride and bridegroom whirled past to Draycot with four greys and postilions.

– 1874 –

WEDNESDAY, 14 JANUARY

To-night my Father told me his reminiscences of my grandfather, old Squire Coleman. 'He was a man of middle height,' he said, 'thin and spare. His hair was grizzled when I knew him. He had a good profile and a fine nose, but his face was the colour of a kite's foot, yellow and unwholesome looking, and his address was rendered unpleasant by a set unmeaning smile. He always said "Sir" to everyone. He dressed in a remarkable way, and looked like a clergyman of the old school in a very large white neckcloth, black coat, white cord breeches, grey gaiters and shoes. He rode a black horse and stooped a good deal over its neck.' (I have heard Edward Little of Lanhill say that my grandfather had the saddle put very far back on the horse and then sat very far back in the saddle). 'I used to go over to Langley occasionally to see your grandfather. Your Aunt Sarah used to ask me to come over and talk to him. One Sunday evening I was sitting with them and Sarah quietly pushed a book towards me. It was a book of sermons. "Shall I read to you?" I asked, opening the book. "If you please, Sir," said the old gentleman with a low and sudden bow and his peculiar set smile. He listened to me but made no remark.'

He was a good and easy landlord, and an upright honourable man in all his dealings. He was a regular attendant at his parish Church, Kington St Michael's, and he was so punctual that the village folks at Kington used to set their clocks by the Squire.

FRIDAY, 30 JANUARY

Drove my Mother to Chippenham. A Radical Candidate has taken us all by surprise. Handel Cossham was nominated this morning. Before daylight the town had broken out with a bad eruption of poisonous yellow bills. We thought Goldney was going to walk over the course without opposition.

THURSDAY, 5 FEBRUARY

This afternoon I went to see the young dragoon Frank Vincent. He is in the 1st Royals and home on furlough of a month from Edinburgh after an illness. He is a fine handsome young fellow as you shall see in a day's march. He said he was fond of Burns, and I read aloud to him Burns' Epistle to a young friend, Andrew Aiken.

FRIDAY, 6 FEBRUARY

To-day the papers brought us good news from Cape Coast Castle. Sir Garnet Wolseley was within a march of Coomassie. The King of Ashantee had sent in his submission and agreed to pay the £200,000 demanded by Sir Garnet.

As I crossed the Common on my way home a form loomed through the thick mist, a labouring man going home from his work, and a voice halloed, 'Stop there till

I see who you be. Is that Mr Frank Kilvert?' It was poor George Bourchier staggering along the worse for drink. I took his hand. 'George,' I said sadly and gently, 'you have had too much.' 'I have, Sir,' he said. 'God forgive me. I cry about it night and morning. I will try to leave it off. God bless you.' The poor wandering sheep.

SATURDAY, ST VALENTINE'S DAY

This afternoon I went to see Frank Vincent, the handsome young Dragoon, once more before he leaves to rejoin his regiment, the 1st Royals at Edinburgh. He is a noble young soldier and singularly attractive and lovable.

MONDAY, 16 FEBRUARY

Greatly troubled by the licentiousness of the school children, especially Harriet Ferris, Mary Grimshaw and Lucy Halliday.

FRIDAY, 20 FEBRUARY

Visited old John Hatherell the sawyer. He began sawing for the Manor the year my great-grandmother old Madame Ashe died in 1823, more than half a century ago, and he has been at the call of the Manor ever since. He had known sore hardships, he said, when the bread was so very dear and he was bringing up a large family. Often he had worked all day up to his knees in water and gone to bed hungry that his children might have bread, and he thought they always had enough.

TUESDAY, 10 MARCH

I found John Gough returned from the Bath United Hospital last Saturday. He was twenty-one years in the army, and fought at Alma and Inkerman where he was wounded. 'No one but themselves who went through it,' he said, 'will ever know what our soldiers endured in the winter of 1854–1855. No firewood but what they cut down or the roots they grubbed up under the fire of the enemy's guns. The coffee served out green to be roasted as the men could over their miserable fires in fragments of shell, and then when burnt or blackened a little pounded with two stones in a piece of canvas or coarse cloth, just something to flavour the water. A little grog and plenty of salt meat, but often no biscuit, and they were afraid to eat much of the salt meat for fear of scurvy. When they came in from the trenches or night fatigue duty, no fire, no straw to lie down on, only a blanket and greatcoat and the mud ankle-deep. On Christmas Day a little piece of butter and two ounces of "figgy pudding" were served to each man out of casks. Tobacco was more precious than gold. If a man was lucky enough to have a pipe he doted on it as if it were Almighty God coming down upon him. Tobacco was so scarce that he hardly dared to put it into the pipe, only a very little bit, and then just two or three draws at a time. Then he stopped the pipe with a bit of rag and put it into his pocket. He could not afford himself more than that at once. If I had had tobacco I could have done with one meal a day. The French soldiers were in plenty while we were starving. The French managed

48

everything well. In our lines there was nothing but shameful mis-management. As many men died of neglect, mis-management, cold, starvation and needless disease as died in battle. The French were four miles nearer to Balaclava and the provision stores, then they had hardy mules, while the English horses dropped under their loads and died by the roadside.'

John Gough said, 'On the Sunday morning November 5th 1854 I was sleeping in the tent. I had been on fatigue duty that night till midnight. About 6 o'clock before daylight a man who slept next to me touched me and said, "Jack, the Rooshians are firing into the camp." I said, "Nonsense, who cares? Let me sleep." However he wouldn't let me be. "It's true," he said with an oath. I wanted to sleep and rapped out a nasty word. It was true enough however and the cannon balls soon came hopping through the camp. Then the bugle sounded "Stand to your arms" and I said, "There is something up then after all." We stood to our arms. It was not daybreak yet and we waited in the shelter of the 4-gun battery that defended our division. Our battery was blazing away at the flashes of the Rooshian guns. This is how we were surprised. There were double sentries on outlying picket duty that night, one to stand and listen while the other walked about and warmed himself. Then he took a turn at listening and the other walked about. When the guard was relieved at 4 o'clock in the morning one of the sentries reported to a captain of the 47th that he could hear a noise like the rattling of waggons coming out of Sebastopol. The sergeant confirmed his report and added that he could hear also that the wheels were muffled. He said the Captain might hear the noise himself if he went down into the ravine. But the Captain laughed at it and took no notice. These waggons were the field pieces and ammunition waggons coming out of Sebastopol to surprise the English and fight the battle of Inkerman. It was the longest battle fought in the war and lasted all day from dawn to dusk.'

MONDAY, 16 MARCH

To-day there was a great gathering at Chislehurst of friends of the exiled Napoleon dynasty to celebrate the coming of age of the Prince Imperial at the age of 18.

Started for Llysdinam by the 8.30 express.

At Three Cocks we waited some time and I fell into talk with one of the Bridgwaters of one of the Porthamal farms who told me about the elections and how at Talgarth Mr de Winton of Maesllwch had been insulted by men kicking round him as a football a rabbit stuffed with bran, in allusion to his propensity for ruining his tenants by keeping vast hordes of rabbits on his estate.

When the train came in from Brecon a tall girl with a fresh colour dressed in deep mourning got out of the train and came towards me. It was Daisy, and her brother John was with her. There was a half sweet, half sad look, a little reproachful in the beautiful kind eyes as she said in a low voice, 'I have been looking out for you such a long time'. Poor child, my poor child.

SATURDAY, 21 MARCH

Left Llysdinam and came to Whitney Rectory.

MONDAY, 23 MARCH

One of the dear old bright happy mornings which seem peculiar and sacred to Whitney Rectory. The sun shone brightly in at the southern window bowered in roses and beautiful creeping plants and the birds chirped and sang in their bowers and I opened my eyes on the familiar view as I looked up the valley of the Wye to the heights of Clyro Hill. Muirbach Hill dawned a soft azure through the tender morning mists. Pretty Louisa Dew bounded up the stairs to meet me with a bright rosy morning face and a lovely kiss, when she heard me leave my room. She will be a noble-looking girl one day and will make somebody's heart ache. She is a very fine girl for her age now and as wild as a hawk but as good as gold, in spite of her dancing spirits. After breakfast a ramble in the garden to see the fruit trees. A white nectarine was in a blaze of purple blossom.

I rode with Henry Dew senior to Clifford Priory to see how Haigh Allen was. We had a scamper back to Whitney Rectory to catch the 1.08 train which was to take me to Hay to stay at Hay Castle.

In the afternoon Mrs Bevan, Mary and I drove to Clyro. As we passed along the old familiar road that I have journeyed over so many times a thousand memories swept over me. Every foot of Clyro ground is classical and sacred and has its story. When we reached the dear old village the children had just come out of the school. I kissed my hand to them, but they seemed as if they could hardly believe their eyes and it was not till after we had alighted at the lodge under the old weeping willow and were walking up the steep drive to Cae Mawr that a ringing cheer came up from the playground.

Mr Morrell was not at home, but Reginald and Winifred came downstairs. They had both forgotten me. Baskerville came to the door and we sat down in the drawing room for a chat.

As we walked down the drive to the carriage renewed cheers came ringing from the school. Mrs Bevan was much amused and Baskerville said to me, 'It is a pity you don't stand for the county. You would have the suffrages of every one here.'

The dear children crowded round the school door. They were a little shy and much grown since I saw them this time last year, but my sweet little Amy was unmistakable and so were the frank sweet eyes of Eleanor Hill.

When we returned to Hay I walked to the almshouses beyond the Brecon turnpike with Mrs Bevan, Alice and Cousie.

The daffodils were nodding in bright yellow clumps in the little garden plots before the almshouse doors. And there a great ecstasy of happiness fell upon me. It was evening when I met her and the sun was setting up the Brecon road. I was walking by the almshouses when there came down the steps a tall slight beautiful girl with a graceful figure and long flowing fair hair. Her lovely face was delicately pale, her features refined and aristocratic and her eyes a soft dark tender blue. She looked at me earnestly, longingly and lovingly, and dropped a pretty courtesy. Florence, Florence Hill, sweet Florence Hill, is it you? Once more. Thank God. Once more. My darling, my darling. As she stood and lifted those blue eyes, those soft dark loving eyes shyly to mine, it seemed to me as if the doors and windows of heaven were suddenly opened. It was one of the supreme moments of life. As I stood by the roadside holding her hand, lost to all else and conscious only of her presence, I was in heaven already, or if still on earth in the body, the flights of golden stairs sloped to my feet and one of the angels had come down to me. Florence, Florence Hill, my darling, my darling. It was well nigh all I could say in my emotion. With one long lingering loving look and clasp of the hand we parted and I saw her no more.

TUESDAY, 24 MARCH, LADY DAY EVE

I went down to the almshouses hoping to see Florence Hill again. Alas, the daffodils were still blowing in the little garden plot, but Florence Hill was gone.

I walked to Clyro by the old familiar fields and the Brecon stile, and when I looked down upon the dear old village nestling round the Church in the hollow at the dingle mouth and saw the fringes of the beautiful woods and the hanging orchards and the green slopes of Penllan and the white farms and cottages dotted over the hills a thousand sweet and sad memories came over me and all my heart rose up within me and went out in love towards the beloved place and people among whom I lived so long and so happily.

I saw a number of the old people. Hannah Whitney was going to the well as of old in her rusty black bonnet tilted on to the top of her head. Mrs Richard Williams was in the churchyard. She had come down from Paradise to trim Mr Henry Venables' grave. Poor Lizzie Powell, a wreck and shadow of the fine blooming girl she was when I saw her last, was crouching up in the sunny window opposite the Vicarage, pale, wasted, shrunken, hollow-eyed and hollow-cheeked, dying of consumption, but with the sanguine and buoyant spirit of that mysterious and fatally deceptive disease, hoping still against hope even with the hand of death upon her. She seemed pleased to see me. She was amusing herself by watching the men at work at the Vicarage building the new garden wall and her brother Charlie among them.

I went to the school to see Evans and his wife and the children. 'We will never forget you,' said one of them. 'I wish,' said Mr Higgins of Clyro Court Farm to me, 'I wish to goodness you were going to stay amongst us. We all love you. We do indeed.'

THURSDAY, 26 MARCH

I slept at Whitney Rectory last night and came to Hay this morning with Henry Dew by the ten o'clock train.

I walked over to Llanthomas to luncheon with Captain John Thomas. Howarth Greenly was there at luncheon and they played quoits after lunch while I walked to the gardens with Charlotte and Fanny. I went back to

Whitney Rectory to sleep as Mr Venables is staying at the Castle. My poor, poor Daisy. When we parted the tears came into her eyes. She turned her face away. I saw the anguish of her soul. What could I do?

SATURDAY, 28 MARCH

Left Hay Castle and returned to Langley after a very pleasant holiday.

TUESDAY, 21 APRIL

At noon I attended a Ruridecanal Conference at the Town Hall in Chippenham.

The Rural Dean, Gray Lawson, unwisely introduced the subject of Contagious Diseases and the enforced surgical examination of suspected women, to ventilate the matter, as he said.

MONDAY, 27 APRIL

This morning came a letter from Mr Henry Moule, Vicar of Fordington, enclosing a note from the Poet, the Revd William Barnes, Rector of Winterbourne Came, near Dorchester, whom I have long wished to see. The Poet says he will be happy to receive a visit from me.

THURSDAY, MAY EVE

This will always be a happy and memorable day in my remembrance.

To-day I visited and made the acquaintance and I hope the friendship of William Barnes, the great idyllic Poet of England. Up at 6 o'clock, breakfast at 6.30, and left Chippenham by the 7.15 train. It was a glorious morning, fresh and exhilarating, as I started on my journey and the unclouded sky shone with a splendid blue over the brilliant green elms and the rich warm golden brown of the oaks. The elms performed a solemn dance circling round each of the fine Church Towers of Somerset as we sped down into Dorset by the windings of the Frome and the elms of Castle Cary. And then the high downs began to rise and we seemed to breathe the sweet salt air as soon as we saw the bold white chalk cliffs that look to the blue sea.

Mr Henry Moule, the Vicar of Fordington for nearly half a century, met me at the Dorchester Station, pointed out to me the great Roman amphitheatre, Maiden Castle, the vallum of the Roman camp, and took me round the beautiful avenues of luxuriant sycamore and chestnut which surround and adorn the town with delightful boulevards foursquare and exquisite shaded walks over-arched by trees which give the place the look of a foreign town.

As we passed along the beautiful water walk and over the hatches between the crystal streams of the Frome and the bright water-meadows below and looked up at the picturesque old high town bosomed in its groves of sycamore and chestnut and tufted with lofty trees we met a lovely girl dressed in deep mourning and walking with her lover, probably a bold handsome artilleryman from the barracks, splendid in blue and gold.

The Vicar told me part of the history of the politics of Fordington, his troubles with the Dorchester people and his struggles with the Council of the Duchy of Cornwall to which the parish of Fordington belongs and from which with great difficulty he has at length wrung some acknowledgement and help in money and improvements.

When the Vicar first came to Fordington he was instrumental, he said, in putting down some low bad races held near Dorchester. This made him very unpopular. For five years none of his family or flock could go into Dorchester without being insulted and baa-ed after like sheep. Twenty or thirty young men stood at the Church gates each Sunday and insulted the pastor and his congregation as they went into Church. And every year all the shrubs and flowers in the garden were rooted up and placed together in the middle of the lawn. All the opposition however had been lived down long ago and now the Vicar seems universally and deservedly respected.

We walked together to the Poet's house, Winterbourne Came Rectory, about a mile from Fordington. The house lies a little back from the glaring white high road and stands on a lawn fringed with trees. It is thatched and a thatched verandah runs along its front. The thatched roof gives the Rectory house the appearance of a large lofty cottage. As we turned in at the iron gates from the high road and went down the gravel path the Poet was walking in the verandah. He welcomed us cordially and brought us into his drawing room on the right-hand side of the door. He is an old man, over seventy, rather bowed with age, but apparently hale and strong. 'Excuse my study gown,' he said. He wore a dark grey loose gown girt round the waist with a black cord and tassel, black knee breeches, black silk stockings and gold buckled shoes.

I was immediately struck by the beauty and grandeur of his head. It was an Apostolic head, bald and venerable, and the long soft silvery hair flowed on his shoulders and a long white beard fell upon his breast. His face was handsome and striking, keen yet benevolent, the finely pencilled eyebrows still dark and a beautiful benevolent loving look lighted up his fine dark blue eyes half hermit, half enchanter.

He is a very remarkable and a very remarkable-looking man, half hermit, half enchanter.

The Poet seemed pleased with my visit and gratified that I had come such a long way to see him. I told him I had for many years known him through his writings and had long wished to thank him in person for the many happy hours his poems had given me. He smiled and said he was very glad if he had given me any pleasure. Frequently stroking his face and his venerable white beard the Poet told me he had composed his poems chiefly in the evening as a relaxation from the day's work when he kept a school in Dorchester.

He was born at [ ] Newton, a son of a small farmer, and in after life when he sat down to amuse himself by writing poetry all the dear scenes and well-remembered events and beloved faces of his youth crowded upon his memory. 'I saw them all distinctly before me,' he said, 'and all I had to do was to write them down. It was no trouble to me, the thoughts and words came of themselves.' He said that some of the names of people and places mentioned in his poems are fictitious, but they all represented real places and persons. The real name of Ellen Brine of Allenburn, he said, was Mary Hames, and the poem was true to the life.

In describing a scene he always had a original in his mind, but sometimes he enlarged and improved upon the original. 'For instance,' he explained, 'sometimes I wanted a bit of water or wood or a hill, and then I put these in.' 'Pentridge by the river,' he said, was a real place, and so were some others. The river was the Stour.

'Once,' said the Poet, 'I had a curious second-sight about a house. It was a farm house in a hollow that I had passed by some time before. I knew nothing about the house or the people, but it haunted me. I saw the place in a vision. Two children, a boy and a girl, were playing in the courtyard. I noticed their features distinctly. The girl ran very swiftly. Afterwards I learnt that just such a boy and girl did live in that house and I am sure that if I were to see these children I should know them by the faces of the children I saw in the vision.'

The Poet is a self-taught man, a distinguished philologist, and is said to understand seventeen languages.

As we walked from Fordington to Came in discussion like friends in council Mr Moule repeated to me some beautiful and touching verses which he had composed when he was in the depths of his great trouble about his poor son Horace. The verses began, 'Lord, I love Thee.' He had sent a copy of them to the Poet who was delighted with them and said it was 'a goodly song from a golden lyre'. Now Mr Moule, who is an universal genius, sat down to the piano in the Poet's drawing room and sang these verses in a sweet deep melodious voice, accompanying himself with a beautiful and appropriate air which he had composed himself and which came to him, he said, like an inspiration. Meanwhile the Poet sat by on an ottoman, stroking his long white beard and glancing round occasionally at me, and clapping his hands softly. He is very musical himself. The walls of the drawing room were almost entirely covered with small oil paintings from floor to ceiling.

At the earnest request of the Vicar the Poet read aloud to us his admirable poem describing how worthy Bloom the Miller went to London to see the great 'glassen house' and how he could not get into the omnibus by reason of his bulk, though he declared he was a poor starved Dorset man. We were all three in roars of laughter. Then to please me he read his beautiful poem called 'Happiness'. It is one of my favourites. He said that 'No So's' means 'No souls', i.e. friends, neighbours. 'No So's.' 'No my friends.' He read in a low voice, rather indistinct and with much feeling. 'I like your pathetic pieces best,' said the Vicar. 'So do I,' said the Poet.

He spoke of Tennyson's *Northern Farmer*. 'Tennyson,' he said, 'even if he did not mean to ridicule the Northern Farmer, at least had no love for him and no sympathy with him.' Which is probably true and a just criticism. The Poet went on to say that in all which he himself had written there was not a line which was not inspired by love for & kindly sympathy with the things and people described. And this is wholly true. All his poems are overflowing with love and tenderness towards the dear scenes and friends of his youth.

He said the cattle calls used to call the cows home at milking time on the Wilts and Dorset dairy farms are the same as those used in Scandinavia.

FRIDAY, MAY DAY

This morning I had a nice letter from the Parshill Barracks from my dear young dragoon Frank Vincent. He says he is trying to follow my advice and to do right though there is a good deal of joking and laughing in the troop at his expense.

Walking up and down the terrace with my Father telling him about the Poet Barnes and discussing with him the advisability of publishing a book of my own poems. I wish to do so. He rather discourages the idea.

SATURDAY, MAY MORROW

Went to Peckingell. Found Austin a little better. He and his wife told me things about the parish which drew aside the veil from my eyes and showed me in what an atmosphere and abyss of wickedness we are living and how little many people are to be trusted whom we thought respectable and good. As the evening sunlight shone bright and searching across the lawn upon the lime the shadows of the leaves were cast strongly upon the tree trunk. The leaves were so brilliant that even their shadows showed a pale faint ghostly green. The shadows looked like the spirits of leaves without the body.

WEDNESDAY, 6 MAY

Though I be tied and bound with the chain of my sin yet let the pitifulness of Thy Great mercy loose me.

TUESDAY, 12 MAY

At the door of the White Lion Hotel in Bath we found a large crowd gathered round the donkey and cart of the nobleman organ-grinder. The disguised nobleman and his organ were putting up at the Hotel and the people were waiting for him to finish breakfast and to come out. No one knows who he is. There are many reports. Some say he is an Irish baronet, some that he is a Lord. It is believed that he has made a wager for £30,000 that he will go about for three years with the same donkey, and live by his earnings. People give him gold in the street and some days it is said he makes as much as £15. Perhaps he has run through one fortune and taken this means of getting another. Or perhaps a fortune of £30,000 was left him to be inherited on this condition.

HOLY THURSDAY, 14 MAY

I met in the drive this morning a poor Frenchman, pale, thin and lank. He said he was a soldier and had been taken prisoner at Sedan in September 1870 and sent to Schleswig Holstein. He was coming up to the Rectory to ask if there were any French people in the neighbourhood who would help him on his way to London. He had been sick and in the Bristol Infirmary and was now on his way home to Strasbourg, his native city. 'My father lived there,' he said, 'but I fear he has gone away now.' I told him I had been to Strasbourg and talked to him about some of the people and places there. A bright pleased look came into his wan sorrowful face for a moment as his old home and native city and the great Cathedral rose before his eyes. But they were far away. He had many a weary mile to limp before he could see the old place again. The eager light faded and the sorrowful wistful suffering look came back into his eyes. He had been twice wounded with a bullet through the thigh and gash down the jaw. He asked me if I had heard 'the chicken cry' (the cock crow) on the clock in Strasbourg Cathedral when he saw St Peter come round with the eleven apostles. He recognized with delight my description of the beautiful woman who kept a photograph shop in the corner house near the front of the Cathedral. 'Ah,' he cried, 'Madame Tournon. But,' he said sadly, 'it is all gone now. It was bombarded in the siege.' 'I hope,' said the poor broken soldier with a sad and deep sigh, 'England will never see such a war as that.'

EXPECTATION SUNDAY, 17 MAY

We shall not have a more lovely Sunday than this has been. The hawthorn bushes were loaded with their sweet May snow, and in the glowing afternoon sun the sheets of buttercups stretched away under the bright elms like a sea of gold.

WHITSUN DAY, 24 MAY

After Church I visited and read to old John Hatherell and Hannah gave me a glass of their excellent parsnip wine.

WHITSUN MONDAY, 25 MAY

At 9 o'clock I went through the mowing grass of the homefield (Cambridge's) to the John Knights' dairy and Fair Rosamund brought me a jug and glass and dipped me up some sweet warm whey as she used to do last summer. She and her mother were breaking curd and making cheese in the great tin tub.

I went down to Greenway Lane Farm by the quiet meadows fragrant with the incense of evening prayers. How sweet and still and pure after the noise and dust and crowd and racket of the town, the fine and smart dresses, the tawdry finery, the flaunting ribbons and the uproar of the cheese market where the band was thundering and the dancers whirling. Here the sweet flowers were blossoming and the only sound was the birds singing very quietly.

WHITSUN TUESDAY, 26 MAY

This afternoon the Rural Dean, Mr Gray Lawson, came to visit and inspect our Church. I met the Churchwardens there at 2.30, and while we were waiting for the Rural Dean Farmer John Bryant and I cut down with a penknife a young elm which was growing at the foot of the Chancel wall beneath the East window and thrust the tree hurriedly into the great laurel bush in the corner which is the receptacle for all rubbish and withered decorations. The dead ivy which has been lately cut has been falling from the Church walls in great dusty rubbishy flakes, but Churchwarden Jacob Knight went to the Church with Emma Halliday yesterday and tidied up a bit. Presently the Rural Dean came and asked many questions, examined the Church within and without narrowly, looked behind the doors and into the books and stamped upon the wooden flooring by the Langley House pew till I feared he might go down into the vaults beneath. He asked about the state of the Tower roof and I offered to go up the shaky old ladder with him but he wisely and hastily declined. As he was walking backwards looking up at the Tower he stumbled backwards among the graves and might have dashed out his brains against the great altar tombs had I not seized him by the arm and held him up. He said our Church was a singular instance of the morning congregation being larger than the afternoon one. Finally he said he had no fault to find and could not pick a hole in our coats.

Croquet, tea and supper at Langley Green.

THURSDAY, 28 MAY

At the dairy it was butter morning and Fair Rosamund was making up the sweet rolls of rich golden butter. Mrs Knight says the butter is so golden at this time of year because the cows eat the buttercups. The reason why the whey is so sweet and wholesome in May and June is because the grass is so full of flowers and young sweet herbs. When I go to the Common Farm to drink whey I think of my grandmother, my mother's mother, Thermuthis Ashe, then a fair beautiful young girl, and how she used to come across the meadows from the Manor house to this very dairy and drink whey here every morning during the sweet May Month.

THURSDAY, 4 JUNE

Went to Bristol with my Mother on a market ticket. She went to see Miss Evans at 6 Oakfield Place, and I to visit Janet Vaughan of Newchurch at the Clergy Daughters' School. On the way up to Great George St where the C.D.S. is I went into the market to buy a nosegay of roses for Janet. As I was sitting in a confectioner's shop between the Drawbridge and College Green eating a bun I saw lingering about the door a bare-footed child, a little girl, with fair hair tossed and tangled wild, an arch espiègle eager little face and beautiful wild eyes, large and grey, which looked shyly into the shop and at me with a wistful beseeching smile. She wore a poor faded ragged frock and her shapely limbs and tiny delicate beautiful feet were bare and stained with mud and dust. Still she lingered about the place with her sad and wistful smile and her winning beseeching look, half hiding herself shyly behind the door. It was irresistable. Christ seemed to be looking at me through the beautiful wistful imploring eyes of the barefooted hungry child. I took her out a bun, and I shall never forget the quick happy grateful smile which flashed over her face as she took it and began to eat. She said she was very hungry. Poor lamb. I asked her name and she told me, but amidst the roar of the street and the bustle of the crowded pavement I could not catch the accents of the childish voice. Never mind. I shall know some day.

In Great George Street, leading out of Park St, I did not know at first where to find the Clergy Daughters' School, but the sound of two or three pianos guided me to the top of the street where stood a large old-fashioned red brick house in a pretty garden. 'Is Miss Vaughan at home?' 'Yes,' and I was shown upstairs into a room overlooking the basin and sweep of the vast smoky town and the dark grey battlements of the Cathedral Tower rising above the avenues of College Green.

Presently I heard a sweet voice singing along the passages and Janet Vaughan came in much grown and with her hair cut short over the forehead, but unchanged in other ways and as sweet and simple and affectionate as ever. She gave me a long loving kiss and we sat down by the open window to talk. Then some ladies came in to see another of the girls of the school and I sent Janet to ask if we might go out into the garden. Leave was given and we went out into a pretty garden at the back of the house with steep sloping lawns and shady winding walks under the trees. Janet took me down a steep path into a secluded walk, dark and shady, at the bottom of the garden, called in the school traditions the 'Poet's Retreat'. Here we walked up and down talking of Clyro and Gilfa and Newchurch and old times. Then girls came out into the garden with their books and work and soon all the shady nooks were full of light dresses and bright pretty faces and pleasant voices.

The walk called the 'Poet's Retreat' was fringed with young trees upon some of which the girls had carved their initials. Upon the stem of a young beech whose bark was grimy black with Bristol smuts I carved Janet's initials J. V. and reluctantly at her earnest request my own R.F.K. above.

SUNDAY, 7 JUNE

I had only three from the village to-night. Cissy Bryant, Emma Halliday and Martha Plank, and I spoke to them about temptation and the Temptation of Christ.

Later the warm soft night was laden with perfume and the sweet scent of the syringa.

TUESDAY, 9 JUNE

Went with my mother and Dora and Lettice Hazel to the Isle of Wight by Salisbury and Stokes Bay. The heat was intense. The Wiltshire downs and Salisbury Plain were white and glaring with drought and chalk and dust in the scorching blinding sun. Everything seemed parched and dried up by the 2 months' drought except some brilliant patches of crimson sainfoin which lighted up the white hot downs and burning Plain with the purple bloom and splendours of heather. At Heytesbury a young handsome intelligent gentlemanly farmer got into the carriage, a man with a ruddy face, light brown hair, merry blue eyes and a white puggery on his hat. We fell into talk about the strike and lock-out in the Eastern Counties and the much vexed labour and wages question. He was on his way to Salisbury Market.

At Shanklin Station there was Lizzie James on the platform smiling to receive Lettice, unchanged since the old Llowes and Clyro days. And there were Gussie and Commerell to meet me and Mrs Cowper Coles outside the Station Gate in her wheel chair given her by the Duchess of Norfolk. So we went up to their house Newstead together and it was very pleasant seeing them all. Mrs Coles has got Newstead on a lease of 999 years. It is a pleasant well-arranged roomy airy house, very light and cheerful, near the edge of the Cliff with glimpses of the bright blue sea between the houses in front.

THURSDAY, 11 JUNE

From the top of the hill how lovely was the view over Brading Harbour, the distant headlands and the white houses along their sides sparkling as clear as crystal in the evening sunshine and the white winged boats moving slowly round the shores (their topsails showing over the green fields) or standing across the calm blue sea.

FRIDAY, 12 JUNE

Bathing yesterday and to-day. Yesterday the sea was very calm, but the wind has changed to the East and this morning a rough and troublesome [sea] came tumbling into the bay and plunging in foam upon the shore. The bay was full of white horses. At Shanklin one has to adopt the detestable custom of bathing in drawers. If ladies don't like to see men naked why don't they keep away from the sight? To-day I had a pair of drawers given me which I could not keep on. The rough waves stripped them off and tore them down round my ancles. While thus fettered I was seized and flung down by a heavy sea which retreating suddenly left me lying naked on the sharp shingle from which I rose streaming with blood. After this I took the wretched and dangerous rag off and of course there were some ladies looking on as I came up out of the water.

THURSDAY, 25 JUNE

Went to London by the 11.5 mail. I left my carpet-bag at the Paddington Cloak Room and went straight to the Academy exhibition at Burlington House which I reached shortly before 4 o'clock. There was a great press of people, 100 or more, round Miss Thompson's famous picture 'Calling the Roll after the battle of Inkerman'. A policeman stands on duty all day by this picture from 10 o'clock till 6 in the evening saying, 'Move on, ladies. Ladies, please move on.'

I met Teddy in the Exhibition and we dined together at the Criterion. Not a bed was to be got at the Great Western Hotel, so I put up at the Norfolk.

FRIDAY, 26 JUNE

Breakfasted with the Venables at 62 Warwick Square.

At ten o'clock I went to Victoria to get a train for the Crystal Palace and the Handel Festival. I found a special train going, but it was so late in starting that we did not reach the Palace till 11.30 when the doors had been open and all the best seats filled for half an hour. I was a long way from the Orchestra and on one side yet I heard all the 28 Choruses admirably. Some of the solos were almost inaudible and all sounded like faint voices coming out of a vast empty distance. Yet the duet 'The Lord is my Strength' between the two sopranos Madame Otto Alvsleben and Madame Lemmens Sherrington was lovely and the duet between the two basses Santley and Signor Foli 'The Lord is a Man of War' was grand, and Sims Reeves sang 'The Enemy said' as splendidly as ever. Madame Lemmens' voice pierced like lightning. To my mind the most marvellous part of this marvellous oratorio is the Chorus describing the plague of darkness. In the thick heavy muffled music you could feel the waves of darkness coming on.

Dined with the Venables at 62 Warwick Square and met Tomkyns Dew and Capt., Mrs, and Miss Hope Adam.

SATURDAY, 27 JUNE

I regret to say that against good advice and wise warning I went to see Holman Hunt's picture of the Shadow of Death. It was a waste of a good shilling. I thought the picture theatrical and detestable and wished I had never seen it. Left London at 2 o'clock and by 7 was visiting the sick people in the village.

THURSDAY, JULY MORROW

As John Couzens was clipping the turf edges of the lawn and beds he told me how for months while he was at work in this place for us, some years ago now, the Devil had tempted him to destroy himself. It came on first quite suddenly in Parson's Ground by the side of the old lane while he was cutting some flower sticks with a bill hook. He threw himself down on the ground in his misery, got away from his bill hook and at last dozed off. His sleep and appetite went from him, and he had no heart nor comfort in his work. He dared not be alone nor within reach of a knife for fear he should cut his throat. He often brought Alice his wife down to be with him while he was at his work and could only rest quiet at night as long as he had his arm round her, for he feared the devil would come and carry him away. He was utterly mierable and one day he went down on his hands and knees behind the great Portugal laurel bush on the lawn by the copper beech (it is cut down since) and cried and prayed terribly and as if his heart would break. This trouble and temptation lasted some months. He did not know what made it come on suddenly then, for he was in good health and spirits. He believed God sent it. For he began to feel how wicked he had been, cursing and swearing and drinking as a young man. The Devil tempted him to destroy himself because he was so wicked. Once when he went up into the loft to throw down some straw he was tempted to make an end of himself by throwing himself down.

'Master told me not to do anything that he didn't tell

me, and not to do anything to myself, but what good were it to tell me that? Mr Headley came here one day and he said to me "Shake it off, John. Shake it off", but what good were that? That were easier said than done. 'Twere easy to say it.' Gradually the trouble and temptation passed away. 'I'm another man now,' he said, 'I've been a different man ever since. But,' he said earnestly, striking his hand upon his shears, 'I wouldn't have any poor creature go through what I went through then, and I wouldn't go through a week of it again for all Squire Ashe's fortune.'

Oh, how little we know of the agonies that are being endured within a few yards of us.

FRIDAY, 3 JULY

I think continually of Daisy. She is seldom out of my thoughts now. I remember her best and she comes to me most often as I saw her at home in March 1873 when I spent a night at her house. I see even now her beautiful white bosom heaving under the lace edging of her dress, and the loose open sleeve falling back from her round white arm as she leaned her flushed cheek upon her hand looking anxiously at me as I coughed. I see her lean forward and hear the low anxious tone in which she asked, 'Does your cough hurt you?' I see her start up and fetch a lamp shade to keep the light from hurting my eyes. Sweet loving Daisy, sweet loving patient faithful Daisy.

SATURDAY, 11 JULY

To-day after 23 years I went to Britford again.

The Vicar has in his house a fine collection of stuffed birds among which are a pair of peregrine falcons which were shot, of all places in the world, on the spire of Salisbury Cathedral. The workmen shot them out of the eight doors at the base of the spire when the steeple was being restored. The Cathedral is generally haunted by peregrines which come from the sea coast cliffs and sit upon the spire whence they can see all the country round and where they think themselves safe. Morris walked with me to the Station in the evening and before us rose the great marvellous spire ever in sight across the flat meadows and beyond the river.

In the town I bought at Decks' a pair of his ten shilling gutta-percha-soled elastic boots.

TUESDAY, 28 JULY

This morning Teddy set up the net and poles in the field just opposite the dining room windows and we began to play 'sphairistike' or lawn tennis, a capital game, but rather too hot for a summer's day.

WEDNESDAY, 29 JULY

Last night the rats most provokingly carried off into their hole the contents of two dishes of apricots which had been gathered yesterday for our croquet party to-day and left on a shelf in the dining-room closet.

When I went to the Farm to drink my whey this morning I told them of our loss. Mrs Knight said that the rats went about overhead at night like race horses, and Mary declared that the walls of their lower cheese-room were lined with rats.

The weather this afternoon was lovely, not too hot, a gentle air moving the silver birch, and bright gleams of sunshine threw beautiful shadows across the lawn and the meadows. The lawn tennis was a successful diversion and afforded a good deal of amusement. About 30 people came, and we were disappointed of some 15.

WEDNESDAY, 5 AUGUST

A splendid romp with Polly Tavener.

THURSDAY, 6 AUGUST

I received this evening a wild strange unhappy note from Susan Strange begging me to come and see her as soon as possible. She was worse and in some trouble of mind about herself. She was also troubled about her daughter Fanny who grieves her sadly by frequently lying and stealing. I told her she must correct the girl in time. 'I do flog her,' she said. 'And the other morning she was a naughty girl and her brother Joseph brought her in to me in her shimmy while I was in bed. I held her hands while Joseph and Charlie whipped her on her naked bottom as hard as ever they were able to flog her.'

FRIDAY, 7 AUGUST

The pastures are burnt to a whitish livid green very pale and ghastly, but the clouds looked stormy and the sky was bright and lurid and wildly tumbled.

SATURDAY, 8 AUGUST

In the afternoon there was a very good cricket match on the Common between Langley Burrell and the Chippenham 2nd eleven. We were beaten by 2 runs, and up to the last moment it was anybody's match. I scored. Just at the end of the match I got a message from Peckingell that little Fanny Strange had suddenly been taken ill and wanted to see me. I went immediately. The child was in bed upstairs. I sat down by the bed and took her little hot hand. She seemed very feverish but was quite sensible and appeared to be much softened and humbled. If so the severe chastisement she has undergone may have had a happy effect and have broken her self-will and cured her of her faults. Her parents very wisely have not spared her nor the rod.

MONDAY, 10 AUGUST

To-day I went to Worthing to be present at Addie Cholmeley's wedding at Findon to-morrow. I left Chippenham at 10.15. At Salisbury I got into the train with a party of people going to South Sea and on the Island. There was an excellent old-fashioned boy in a chocolate jacket with a shiny peaked cap and a white ruffled frill standing out all round his neck like Punch's dog, a very refreshing sight in these degenerate days.

As we journeyed along the fair Sussex shore between the plain and the sea the gleaners were busy in the golden stubbles, the windmills whirled their arms in the fresh sea breeze, the shocks of corn circling changed places swiftly like a dance of fairies, and Chichester steeple rose fair and white far over the meads.

I thought Worthing Station pretty, light and elegant, with its vandyked glass roofs over the platforms. I drove at once to 11 Church Terrace, Mrs Smallwood's, the lodgings which Adelaide has taken and which she gives up to John Cholmeley and myself while she is at Findon Rectory for 2 days for the wedding. After tea and mutton chops I went out to the beach to view the town and the sea. I walked westward to the end of the esplanade. A heavy wrack of dark cloud drove up from the west promising a stormy night and I turned my solitary steps homeward or lodging-ward. And all the while, sweet Kathleen Mavourneen, thou wert in Worthing and near to me and I knew it not. But then I knew not thee, nor what happiness was in store for me in God's Providence. But had I not been a stricken fool I should have gone to Vaynona and been rewarded by seeing thee there.

TUESDAY, 11 AUGUST

Addie Cholmeley's wedding day. This may be one of the happiest and most important days in my life, for to-day I fell in love at first sight with sweet Kathleen Mavourneen.

At the time appointed Miss Cholmeley came to the door with her brother Waldo and drove me to Findon, John Cholmeley coming afterwards with his sister Clara (Mrs Heanley). After a pleasant drive of 4 miles the carriage put us down at the Churchyard gate. In the Church we found Robert Heanley, the best man. I took a fancy to him at once for his pleasant frank open face. After we had been waiting in Church for some time he advised me to go out into the porch to watch the bridesmaids arrive and to be made acquainted with the young lady who was to be my companion for the day, I being one of the five groomsmen. So I went, little thinking whom I was to meet, and what a difference it would make to me.

A pretty bevy of bridesmaids was seen coming up the path in white and green. 'There,' said Miss Sarah Cholmeley to me, 'there is your bridesmaid, the tall dark one behind on the right hand side.' They came up and we were introduced. She was a tall handsome girl with very dark hair, eyebrows and eyelashes, and beautiful bright grey eyes, a thin high aristocratic nose, a sweet firm rosy mouth, beautiful white teeth, a well developed chin, a clear complexion and fresh colour. That was Kathleen Mavoureen as I first saw her. I noticed afterwards that she wore pearl earrings.

[The wedding is described.]

In the afternoon almost all the wedding party went up to that fine clump and height of the Downs called Chanctonbury Ring. Part of the way we drove and we walked up the steepest part. Kathleen was still my sweet companion. Under the lee of the clump I spread my coat on the turf and we sat there together on the hillside apart from the rest and looked over the wide and glorious landscape, bright plain and green pasture, blue hill and golden corn and stubble fields, till she could see over rich and variegated plain the white line of the Grand Stand on Epsom Downs some 30 miles away. And there we sat and talked and looked into each other's eyes and there I fell in love and lost my heart to the sweetest noblest kindest bravest-hearted girl in England, Kathleen Mavourneen. Chanctonbury, sweet Chanctonbury, thou wilt always be a green and beautiful spot in my memory. How sweet she was, how simple, kind, unaffected and self-unconscious, how thoughtful for everyone but herself, and so careful lest Montie on his crutches should trip over the roots in the wood. She spoke of her favourite *In Memoriam* and told me some of her difficulties and how deeply she regretted the enforced apparent idleness of her life, and I loved her a hundred times better for her sweet troubled thoughts and honest regretful words.

'I feel,' she said, 'as if I had known you a long time through your letters to Adèle. She used to talk of you a great deal to me. She was very fond of you.' I felt as if our souls were drawing together on the hillside and I thanked God that in His love and mercy He had brought us face to face and made our paths to cross. In His great mercy may they unite and remain one for ever. Oh, that this companionship of a day may grow and ripen into a companionship for life. Several little things happened during the day which led me to hope that she did not dislike me. She asked me to gather her a bunch of purple heather from the hillside. As we were driving home down the steep green down the wind blew cold and fresh as it met her, and she looked so sweet and grateful when I wrapped my coat round her to keep her warm.

When I was talking to Adelaide in her hearing in the drawing room about the Herefordshire wedding to which I was going, Kathleen turned sharply round as if she were pained and did not want me to go. What conceit. As if she cared. But love can live on very slender nourishment.

We came back from Chanctonbury Ring to Findon Rectory to high tea, after which I had a happy hour with Kathleen in the drawing room. She and Jessie Russell asked me to become a member of their Mutual Improvement Society, and we arranged all the details.

When the party broke up and I was returning to Worthing with Mrs Heanley and Miss Penelope Cholmeley, Kathleen kissed her mother fondly at the door and said to me, 'If you are going in my mother's carriage please not to let her talk, it isn't good for her.' Then she took me back into the dining room to shew me one of the pretty ornaments of the wedding cake that I had not seen at breakfast. After which she gave me one of the silver-leaved white orange flowers off the cake, and what I prized more than all she gave me unasked one precious stephanotis flower out of one of the bridal bouquets, a flower that I will keep till we are married if that should be God's will for us, and in any case until I die. At breakfast she had said to me as we rose from table, 'Take care of that cracker, don't let it be lost'. And I have that too and a motto out of one of the crackers which we pulled together and which she gave me to read. We parted with a long close warm clasp of hands that I felt was friendly and hoped might be affectionate.

We had a dark silent drive back to Worthing. No one spoke. We were all full of our own thoughts.

WEDNESDAY, 12 AUGUST

In the night there was a torrent of rain but the morning broke clear and beautiful. I went out early into the town before breakfast and walked along the beach. Sea and town and everything were sparkling bright and clean after the storm in the clear shining after the rain. The bathing machines were running down into the sea, the sailors were busy about their boats and nets, and the sailors' wives sat working in the sunshine by their husbands' boats. Children were trooping out on to the beach before breakfast and everything looked bright, cheerful, busy and happy.

After breakfast I parted with John Cholmeley and wrote a note to Adelaide telling her of my love for Kathleen.

I left Worthing at 9.27. How much has happened since I entered it a few short hours ago, and how entirely everything is changed for me. Since I have been in love with Kathleen everything seems bright and beautiful, and I feel that I can love God and man better than I ever could before.

SUNDAY, 16 AUGUST

This morning I had a kind loving letter from Adelaide giving me some hope and encouragement about Kathleen which made me very happy for the rest of the day. I wrote a long letter to her on the same subject.

FRIDAY, 21 AUGUST

Went with Dora to Clifton to spend the day with Adelaide at 1 Carlton Place. After an early dinner we went out on to the Clifton down and while the rest of the party accompanied by Anna went down into the slush and mire and darkness of the Giant's Cave, Adelaide and I sat on one of the seats on the edge of the Cliff looking down upon the Suspension Bridge talking of Kathleen Mavourneen. I shall never now see the Suspension Bridge from the Cliff without thinking of Kathleen.

MONDAY, 31 AUGUST

When I went out with Jock this morning to walk across the Common before breakfast there as usual were the three white tiddling lambs lying round the white gate. Immediately the three bold white lambs began to play with the black dog, to hunt him about and butt him sportively, while the dog with his ears laid back pretended to be afraid of the lambs, ran away from them, bounded back, faced them and occasionally took one of them by the ear.

I love to wander on these soft gentle mournful autumn

days, alone among the quiet peaceful solitary meadows, tracing out the ancient footpaths and mossy overgrown stiles between farm and hamlet, village and town, musing of the many feet that have trodden these ancient and now well nigh deserted and almost forgotten ways and walking in the footsteps of the generations that have gone before and passed away.

MONDAY, 7 SEPTEMBER

Went to the Farm, drank whey in the dairy, paid Jacob Knight £2 2s. for the use of the cricket ground on the Common, and took a game fowl's egg to Elizabeth Knight. As I returned I heard in Greenway Lane the old familiar sound once so common, the sound of the flail on the barn floor. I had not heard it for years. I looked in at the barn door and found a man threshing out his barley.

[After a round of visits Kilvert arrives at Clyro.]

SUNDAY, 13 SEPTEMBER

I asked leave of the Vicar to go to Bettws Chapel this afternoon to preach in the old Chapel once more that I might have an opportunity of seeing some of my dear old friends.

As I came down the deep hollow lane between the Bird's Nest Dingle and Court Evan Gwynne I heard voices of women on the high bank above me coming up the field path home from evening Church. Then my own name struck my ear. 'They do say Mr Kilvert was in Church this morning,' said a familiar voice in the dusk. 'Here he is,' I called laughingly from below. It was pretty and touching to see the delight of the women. They stretched their hands down lovingly to clasp mine and seemed as if they would have broken through the hedge in their eagerness and enthusiasm. 'Well,' cried a tall handsome woman, 'well, I did never see such a thing. I was just speaking your name and here you are. I have thought of you,' she added lovingly, 'I have thought of you fresher this week than for a long time. And here you are come.'

MONDAY, 14 SEPTEMBER

Villaging in the morning.

At noon I started with Morrell and the Vicar and Curate (Prickard and Trumper) to walk to Aberedw across the hills. It was one of the loveliest days I ever saw and the mountains were in all their beauty of light and tender blue. We sat to take our luncheon upon the turf of the Beacons beside a tinkling rivulet over against Llanbedr Church. A sweet fresh wind was moving upon the hills and brilliant gleams of green and purple cloud shadows were flying upon the great landscape. In the narrow green sunny lanes the nuts still hung from the hazel tree and a small farmer driving a herd of fat red oxen put us into the right way with the beautiful courtesy of Radnorshire. Below us Bychllyn Pool lay in its hollow like a silver shield and the heather was blooming purple upon the hills. Over the rolling moor rose the pointed cone of Penpicca Hill and we came down into the grand amphitheatre which embosoms the twin valleys and the meeting of the sweet waters of the Edw and the Wye. From Aberedw we walked by the river side and the Nith to Erwood where we took the train to Hay.

WEDNESDAY, 16 SEPTEMBER

Visited poor Amy Powell who is in deep grief for the recent loss of her daughter Lizzie. Went to see Gina Beaven, the Mintons, Catherine Williams, Naomi Williams, John, Mrs Thomas, Miss Morgan at the Post Office, Mrs John Powell, Mrs Jones and James Jones at the Infant School, Jones the shoemaker and Caroline Price. In the afternoon I went to see Miss Chaloner, Hannah Whitney, Ada Chaloner, Mrs Williams at the Lower House, old John Morgan the soldier at the Bronith, Mrs Watkeys, and then on to Upper Cabalva. Annie had come down from Llywn Gwillim. Mr Dyke, Willie and Johnnie came home from the sheep fair at Hay, with Mr Wall. Lucretia Wall came down from the Chapel, and we had a merry tea party.

THURSDAY, 17 SEPTEMBER

Went to Llysdinam. I never had a lovelier journey up the lovely valley of the Wye. A tender beautiful haze veiled the distant hills and woods with a gauze of blue and silver and pearl. It was a dream of intoxicating beauty. I saw all the old familiar sights, the broad river reach at Boughrood flashing round the great curve in the sunlight over its hundred steps and rock ledges, the luxuriant woods which fringe the gleaming river lit up here and there by the golden flame of a solitary ash, the castled rock-towers and battlements and bastions of the Rocks of Aberedw, the famous rocky wooded gorge through the depths of which the narrow mountain stream of the Edw rushed foaming to its Aber to meet the Wye, the house of Pant Shoni gleaming white through the apple-laden orchard trees, the green Castle Mount, Llanvareth Church half hidden by its great dark yew, the sudden bend of the river below Builth, the Yrfon mouth above the little ancient town, and last but not least the grey-towered house of Llysdinam sitting on its green sunny hill backed by dark woods, and looking towards the river and the mountains of the South.

[Kilvert returns to Langley Burrell.]

THURSDAY, 24 SEPTEMBER

This afternoon. I walked over to Kington St Michael by Langley Burrell Church and Morrell Lane and the old Mausoleum and Langley Ridge and the Plough Inn. It was a day of exceeding and almost unmatched beauty, one of those perfectly lovely afternoons that we seldom get but in September or October. A warm delicious calm and sweet peace brooded breathless over the mellow sunny autumn afternoon and the happy stillness was broken only by the voices of children blackberry gathering in an adjoining meadow and the sweet solitary singing of a robin.

As I drew near Kington I fell in with a team of red oxen, harnessed, coming home from plough with chains rattling and the old ploughman riding the fore ox, reminding me vividly of the time when I used to ride the oxen home from plough at Lanhill.

MONDAY, MICHAELMAS EVE

This morning I had a kind thoughtful letter from Adelaide from 1 Carlton Place, Clifton, saying she thought it selfish not to let me know that Kathleen Mavourneen is within an hour's journey of me, staying with her, and asking me if I could trust myself to go down and see her and spend a day with her. So I am going and I shall see her again.

THURSDAY, OCTOBER DAY

This morning I went to Bristol to spend the day with Adelaide and Kathleen Mavourneen at 1 Carlton Place, Clifton. I took Adelaide down a basket of flowers and fruit, plums and grapes, and soon Kathleen Mavourneen was busied arranging the flowers in vases. She was looking very pretty and was most sweet and kind in her manner.

After a heavy storm the weather cleared and we projected a visit to St Mary Redcliffe on my way to the Station. Adelaide, Kathleen, Ella and I went down in a cab, a merry laughing party. The Church is still under repair, the roof of the nave being now nearly restored. The verger said the Church had been under the workmen's hands for the last 45 years, a thousand pounds being spent every year. We struck the sounding pillars near the Confessional, but they do not ring as they did formerly. Kathleen, Ella and I ascended the spiral staircase to the Muniments Room and saw the old wormeaten remnants of the chests in which Chatterton 'the marvellous boy, the sleepless soul that perished in his pride' averred that he had discovered the poems of Rowley the monk.

And there in the great windy dusty room as we looked out through the mullions of the glassless windows over the murky smoky misty city there came a sweet reminiscence of the sunny hillside of Chanctonbury Ring on the afternoon of the Findon wedding day. It was a reminiscence of Sir Walter Raleigh's Cloak which on that day had done good and sweet service, in the carriage and on the turf of the hillside.

FRIDAY, 2 OCTOBER

Prostrate with neuralgia.

Our ginger plant is now in magnificent blossom, a curious tendrilled flower like an orchis, and the scent so strong that we have been obliged to turn the plant from the dining into the drawing room and thence into the hall.

SUNDAY, 4 OCTOBER

Much better, but still weak.

This morning I had a kind letter from Adelaide from Clifton and Kathleen enclosed some hymns she had copied out for me and some references to passages in our favourite *In Memoriam*.

MONDAY, 5 OCTOBER

Hannah Hood uses a curious word for 'gulp'. She says, 'I took two or three "glutches" of port wine.'

This month there is in the *Cornhill Magazine* an article on Crabbe's poetry. My Father says he remembers staying with the Longmires at Wingfield about the year 1830. They took him one afternoon to a book sale at Trowbridge, of which parish the poet Crabbe was then Rector. In the evening the whole party adjourned to the Rectory, where they found Crabbe playing whist with three friends in a large drawing room. Crabbe's son (who was acting as his father's curate) was present, a keen-looking laughable man, an exaggerated likeness of Henry Dew. He came forward to receive the visitors while Crabbe continued his game. My Father describes the poet as being a small plain insignificant-looking old man, bald and with a whitish yellow complexion.

SATURDAY, 17 OCTOBER

This evening I had a kind note from Mrs Heanley enclosing some of Kathleen's Mutual Improvement Questions and Answers and better still a beautiful and thoughtful comparison in dear Kathleen's own words of the views from Clifton Downs and Chanctonbury Ring. Her sweet pure thoughts came to me at a time when I sorely needed them and they have done me much good. But they show me only still more clearly what I have often felt before, how much nobler and holier her thoughts are than mine, and how much higher she has climbed up the hill than I have done. Yet I am trying to follow, and I thank God that I ever knew her and (I hope I may say) won her friendship. She has indeed been, unconsciously, a good and guardian angel to me. Sweet Kathleen Mavourneen, God bless thee.

FRIDAY, 23 OCTOBER

When the Squire came to see John Hatherell last Sunday he reminded the old man of the nights they patrolled the roads together 45 years ago during the machine-breaking riots. Robert Ashe led a patrol of six men one half the night, and Edward Ashe headed another patrol of equal strength the other half. One night when Robert Ashe was patrolling the village with his men and keeping watch and guard against the machine-breakers and rioters, who were expected from Christian Malford and other villages, he seized by mistake old Mr Eddels, taking him in the dark for a machine-breaker or incendiary. The old man had come out at night in the innocence of his heart to get some straw from his rickyard.

WEDNESDAY, 28 OCTOBER

This morning we held a family conclave and indignation meeting about the Church singing. At last we resolved that as Mr Ashe has practically dismissed George Jeffries from his post as leader of the singing and rendering it impossible for the singing to go on upon the old footing, we must rather than give up singing in the service have a harmonium or some instrument in the Church, whether he likes it or not. We are prepared to give up the living and leave the place should we be obliged to do so rather than submit any longer to this tyranny. I don't think it will come to this. No such luck as to leave Langley. We should all be better and happier elsewhere, more independent and what is most important of all we should have more self-respect. For my own part I should for many reasons be glad and thankful to go. I don't know how it will end. I suppose I shall stay here as long as my Father lives, no longer.

THURSDAY, 29 OCTOBER

At 8.30 this morning we sent the harmonium to the Church on the trucks with John and George and soon after 10 o'clock Fanny and I followed to see where it ought to be placed and hear how it sounded. Though a small instrument it quite filled the Church with sound. We placed it in the Baptistery close by the Font. This morning was an epoch in the history of Langley Church and the first sound of an instrument within the old walls, an event and sensation not soon to be forgotten. How this innovation, necessary though it has become, will be received by the Squire no one can tell. He has forced us to do it himself and opened the way for the change by dismissing George Jeffries, the chief singer, from his post of leader of the Church singing, but we expect some violence of language at least.

Carried Annie Savine a rice pudding and some old linen to bind up her face and Elizabeth Bourchier's leg.

SUNDAY, ALL HALLOWMAS DAY 1874

All has gone off well. Fanny played the harmonium nicely and the singing was capital. The congregation were delighted and some of them could hardly believe their ears and the Squire said nothing for or against, but he came to Church twice.

TUESDAY, 3 NOVEMBER

This morning between breakfast and luncheon I walked up to Bowood to see the beeches by way of the Cradle Bridge, Tytherton Stanley and Studley Hill. I went into Bowood Park by the Studley Gate and turned sharp to the left down a drive that brought me soon into the very heart and splendour of the beeches. As the sun shone through the roof of beech boughs overhead the very air seemed gold and scarlet and green and crimson in the deep places of the wood and the red leaves shone brilliant standing out against the splendid blue of the sky. A crowd of wood pigeons rose from the green and the misty azure hollows of the plantation and flapped swiftly down the glades, the blue light glancing off their clapping wings. I went by the house down to the lakeside and crossed the water by the hatches above the cascade. From the other side of the water the lake shone as blue as the sky and beyond it rose from the water's edge the grand bank of sloping woods glowing with colours, scarlet, gold, orange and crimson and dark green. Two men were fishing on the further shore of an arm of the lake and across the water came the hoarse belling of a buck while a coot fluttered skimming along the surface of the lake with a loud cry and rippling splash.

To eye and ear it was a beautiful picture, the strange hoarse belling of the buck, the fluttering of the coot as she skimmed the water with her melancholy note, the cry of the swans across the lake, the clicking of the reels as the fishermen would up or let out their lines, the soft murmur of the woods, the quiet rustle of the red and golden drifts of beech leaves, the rush of the waterfall, the light tread of the dappled herd of deer dark and dim glancing across the green glades from shadow into sunlight and rustling under the beeches, and the merry voices of the Marquis's children at play.

Why do I keep this voluminous journal? I can hardly tell. Partly because life appears to me such a curious and wonderful thing that it almost seems a pity that even such a humble and uneventful life as mine should pass altogether away without some such record as this, and partly too because I think the record may amuse and interest some who come after me.

WEDNESDAY, 4 NOVEMBER

This evening I had my first Wednesday winter evening service and lecture at the school and reviewed the events of the last seven months, the funeral of Dr Livingstone, the visit of the Czar, the Spanish war, the Thorpe railway disaster, the explosion of benzaline and gunpowder on the Regent's Park Canal, the Bengal Famine, shipwrecks and collisions at sea, the *Cherson*, the *Candahar* and *Kingsbridge*, etc.

SUNDAY, 8 NOVEMBER

At Morning Church there was a pleasant sight. Vincent, the Langley Burrell policeman, who is not often able to attend service was there with all his sons and amongst them Frank the fine handsome young dragoon in his bright scarlet uniform home on furlough.

After morning service Dora went out to Mr Ashe in the churchyard and asked him to head the subscription list to buy a new harmonium. He said that neither he nor any of his household should give a farthing for he disapproved of any music in a church beside the human voice and he also apprehended a chronic difficulty in finding some one to play the instrument. I walked from church with dear Sarah Hicks to her house at the Pound. 'Oh,' she said earnestly, with indignant tears swelling in her beautiful large dark eyes, 'oh, it's a comfort to know that there's a time coming when no one will be able to reign over us and when we shall be as good as those who are so high and proud over us now.' Patience, dear Sarah, patience a little while longer. And then –

MONDAY, 9 NOVEMBER, TEDDY'S BIRTHDAY

Dora went to the Woods and to the John Knights' this morning collecting subscriptions for the harmonium. Mr Wood was from home, but the Knights came forward most handsomely. Every member of the family at home put down his or her name and the sum of their contributions amounted to a guinea. I was greatly touched for I know it is quite as much as they can afford. This afternoon I went to the Barrow with the subscription paper and left it there. When I stated that the Squire had declined to give anything young John Bryant burst into a scornful laugh. The Churchwarden took his eldest son Tom aside to the window to look over the subscription list in the fading light and promised to return it tomorrow. Alice Couzens volunteered sixpence and said that other cottagers would like to help.

TUESDAY, 10 NOVEMBER

The subscription list was returned from the Barrow at breakfast time this morning signed with the names of almost all the Bryant family, their subscriptions amounting in all to £1. This is very kind and liberal for they are not rich and they have had heavy losses this summer, three cows amongst the rest. Called on the Lawrences to ask for a subscription for the harmonium. They were very kind and readily gave me 12/6. Then Mrs Lawrence burst forth with a harangue and her views upon Church Music. 'I like the music in Church. I don't like everything to be so melancholy, melancholy. I had rather hear a good whistle in Church than nothing. I knew two young ladies who whistled beautifully a first and a second. No, they didn't whistle in Church.'

WEDNESDAY, 11 NOVEMBER, MARTINMAS DAY

We are in trouble at the school now because a few days ago Mr Ashe came angrily in to Miss Bland the school-mistress and ordered her always to keep all three windows and the door of the schoolroom open during schooltime, except in very cold weather when one window might be shut. He said in a fierce determined way. 'This is my school and I will have my word attended to. If you don't do as I tell you, Miss Bland, instead of being your friend I'll be your enemy.' What a speech for an elderly clergyman. It is almost incredible. And there are the poor little children crying with the cold. Cruel. Barbarous. And of course the parents are indignant and the numbers of the children falling off.

THURSDAY, 12 NOVEMBER

Mrs Banks said the Squire had been very unkind to her. He had sent her some rough notes about the cream being bad and complained fiercely of the pigs straying into the woods.

This evening in reply to my letter to Llysdinam I got a most kind letter from Mrs Venables enclosing £2.2 for our harmonium, £1 from herself, 10/- from Mrs Henry Venables, 6/- from dear little Katie, and Mr Venables who got the P.O.O. made the money even. What a difference in the spirit and atmosphere of Llysdinam and Langley House.

MONDAY, 16 NOVEMBER

This afternoon I called at Rawlings for the Matthews'
subscription to the harmonium, 10/- heartily given and
more cordially offered if wanted. Alice Matthews said
quaintly, 'How strange it is that the Squire is such a
distant man about music.'

THURSDAY, 19 NOVEMBER

At last the new harmonium has come. Mr Rooke the
maker brought it up from Weymouth to-day. Our churchwarden Jacob Knight, his uncle Thomas Knight, and his
cousin Ralph Knight and I assembled at the Church
between one and two o'clock and there we had to wait
an hour and half before the harmonium came up from
the Station in a low cart under the care of Mr Rooke,
our John, and one of the Company's men.

At last the harmonium hove in sight and with a long
pull and strong pull and a pull all together we carried it
from the road to the porch and there unpacked it. The
instrument was placed in a little seat behind the pillar at
the west end of the Church whereby taking out the back
of the seat we made a little chamber for it.

SUNDAY, 22 NOVEMBER

A raw cold foggy frosty morning and to-day we had
the first fire in Church. The Squire came in with Mrs
Ashe and Syddie as usual, but as soon as he saw or
smelt the fire in the stove he turned round and went

hastily out again. This morning our new harmonium was played in Church for the first time. It is a beautiful instrument with a soft sweet tone and Fanny managed it very well. I think the people were pleased and Mrs Ashe and Syddie whom we saw after the service said they liked the instrument very much. The singing of the Choir and the congregation in the Old Hundredth Psalm and the Trinity Hymn was especially good and hearty.

TUESDAY, 24 NOVEMBER

In the afternoon I walked over to Kington St Michael to see the sick Vicar. He was better and downstairs in the drawing room. He was as full of life and fun as ever and told me he had heard his mother say that my great-great-grandmother, old Mrs Martyn of Kennet, once sent to my great-grandmother, Mrs Ashe of Langley Burrell, her daughter, a pair of earrings by broad-wheeled waggon, the only public conveyance in those days.

TUESDAY, DECEMBER DAY

My Mother writes from Monnington that William had just been at a clerical meeting at Mr Phillott's, the Rector of Stanton-on-Wye, and came back not very deeply impressed by the brilliancy of some of the Herefordshire Clergy.

She mentions too a story which seems almost incredible but which she states is well known to be true. Mr Ormerod, the Rector of Presteign, who has a living of £1000 a year but who is nevertheless always over head and ears in debt, has every Sunday two Celebrations of the Holy Communion at which he always puts upon the plate his pocket knife by way of alms, saying that he has no change. After service he returns his knife to his pocket, but (it is stated) invariably forgets to *redeem* it.

FRIDAY, 4 DECEMBER

As we went down to Lacock last evening we fell in with Mr Roach the Vicar standing at his gate. He walked into the village with us saying he was cold and sorrowful, for his daughter had just returned from Chippenham with the sad news that in the terrible gale of last Sunday morning the *La Plata* telegraph cable-laying ship foundered after springing a leak and went down off Ushant in the Bay of Biscay with sixty souls, amongst whom was the Captain of the ship, Captain Dudden, who married poor Georgia Spencer. The Spencers are in deep grief and they dare not tell the poor young widow of her loss as she is expecting her first child and very delicate. It is very remarkable that Captain Dudden sailed on this fatal voyage with a strong and sad reluctance, weighed down by a dark and sorrowful presentiment that he would never return. He made his poor young wife promise that she would not look at a newspaper till after her confinement and he told Lloyd's agent if and when the ship went down to telegraph, not to his wife, but to his father-in-law at Chippenham. Yet then there was no presage of a storm.

THURSDAY, 10 DECEMBER

In consequence of an invitation from Adelaide Cholmeley I went to Bristol this morning and spent a happy
merry day with her and Ella and Jessie Russell who is
staying with them at 1 Carlton Place. Adelaide was
very kind and encouraged me very much about matters
in Lincolnshire. She said, 'Katie likes you very much.'
Katie, dear Katie, wanted very much to write to me and
could not understand why she should not. 'Why,' she
said, remonstrating with her Mother, 'Jessie writes to
him.' Dear Katie, she is as brave and true as steel.
Well, patience, patience, hope and wait. The course
of true love never did run smooth. But I do long and
yearn to see her again. Adelaide has brought back
from Lincolnshire a charming vignette of Katie. It is a
grand, noble face, very handsome and something much
better than handsome. Adelaide lent me her old photograph of Katie in her riding dress to go on a long visit to
Langley.

Jean Russell is a capital girl, nice, bright, lively and
amusing and perfectly unaffected. After our early dinner
she, Ella and I went for a walk over the Suspension
Bridge along the edge of Nightingale Valley and through
the Leigh Woods beautiful even in winter. Adelaide was
obliged to stay at home with a cold. It was a bright frosty
day and we had a merry happy walk, Jessie in fits of
laughter at the story of my visit to the young ladies'
school in Great George St when the Lady Principal was
horrified to discover that I was not as she had thought
'quite an old gentleman'. Reached home at 7 o'clock in

time for the night school, bringing our children a cocoa nut to their great delight.

SATURDAY, 12 DECEMBER

There is a beauty in the trees peculiar to winter, when their fair delicate slender tracery unveiled by leaves and showing clearly against the sky rises bending with a lofty arch or sweeps gracefully drooping. The crossing and interlacing of the limbs, the smaller boughs and tender twigs make an exquisitely fine network which has something of the severe beauty of sculpture, while the tree in summer in its full pride and splendour and colour of foliage represents the loveliness of painting. The deciduous trees which seem to me most graceful and elegant in winter are the birches, limes, beeches.

MONDAY, 14 DECEMBER

This evening at 5 o'clock I took 21 of our schoolchildren into Chippenham to the Temperance Hall to see a Panorama of the African travels of Dr Livingstone. One of the most favourite pictures with the children was the Funeral of Dr Livingstone in Westminster Abbey. The Abbey was first shown empty. Then by a slight dioramic effect or dissolving view the open space in the Nave gradually melted into the forms of the funeral party, Dean Stanley reading the service and the mourners grouped round the flower wreath-covered coffin.

THURSDAY, 17 DECEMBER

This morning after long suspense and waiting we were thankful to receive the happy news that dear Thersie was safely confined of a fine boy at Monnington Rectory at 10 p.m. Tuesday, 15th December. Thank God for this and all His mercies.

THURSDAY, CHRISTMAS EVE

Writing Christmas letters all the morning. In the afternoon I went to the Church with Dora and Teddy to put up the Christmas decorations. Dora has been very busy for some days past making the straw letters for the Christmas text. Fair Rosamund and good Elizabeth Knight came to the Church to help us and worked heartily and well. They had made some pretty ivy knots and bunches for the pulpit panels and the ivy blossoms cleverly whitened with flour looked just like white flowers.

The churchwarden Jacob Knight was sitting by his sister in front of the roaring fire. We were talking of the death of Major Torrens on the ice at Corsham pond yesterday. Speaking of people slipping and falling on ice the good churchwarden sagely remarked, 'Some do fall on their faces and some do fall on their rumps. And they as do hold their selves uncommon stiff do most in generally fall on their rumps.'

I took old John Bryant a Christmas packet of tea and sugar and raisins from my Mother. The old man had covered himself almost entirely over in his bed to keep himself warm, like a marmot in its nest. He said, 'If I live till New Year's Day I shall have seen ninety-six New Years.' He said also, 'I do often see things flying about me, thousands and thousands of them about half the size of a large pea, and they are red, white, blue and yellow and all colours. I asked Mr Morgan what they were and he said they were the spirits of just men made perfect.'

SATURDAY, S. STEPHEN'S DAY

This morning, soon after breakfast, Lucy Halliday came up to ask me to go and see Hannah Williams as she was worse. I went immediately and found her in a sad state of suffering. The proud haughty beautiful face was laid low at last and flushed with pain, the thick black hair contrasting vividly with the white pillow as the poor child tossed her shapely head, rolling wearily from side to side seeking, seeking rest, and finding none. Then for a minute she lay silent with closed eyes and flushed cheek buried in the pillows, and then once more began the bitter pain and the weary moaning. 'Oh, mother, oh, mother.' Her father knelt at the foot of the bed holding her feet tenderly, for the agony was in her legs and feet. Last Wednesday night while carrying a bucket of water from the well she slipped upon the icy path and fell heavily upon her back. We fear her spine was injured for though she suffers acute pain in her legs she cannot move them. The poor wild beautiful girl is stopped in her wildness at last, and perhaps by the finger of God.

I saw Hannah Williams again this afternoon and sat a

while by her bedside repeating the Evening Hymn 'Sun of my soul'.

This evening Teddy left us to return to London. A sharp frost, the stars brilliant and the roads glassed with ice. I went with him to the white gate where we parted and I turned off across the dark icy fields towards the village to try to read Hannah Williams to sleep. She had sunk to sleep two minutes before I got there, said her mother, coming noiselessly and gratefully to the head of the stairs. The light shone through the night from the sick girl's chamber window, the night was still, an owl hooted out of the South and the mighty hunter Orion with his glittering sword silently overstrode the earth.

SUNDAY, CHILDERMAS EVE

Before I went to Church this morning I went to see Hannah Williams. Before I reached the cottage I heard the poor girl's distressing moans. They were moving her in her bed and it was heartrending to hear her. After tea I went to see Hannah and try to read the poor child to sleep. I stayed there an hour or more turning her in bed every quarter of an hour. She says I turn her and lift her better than any one else.

MONDAY, CHILDERMAS DAY

To-day we heard by a short telegram of the awful calamity of the burning of the emigrant ship *Caspatria* near the Cape of Good Hope bound for New Zealand. Four hundred and forty persons burnt in her. One boat reached St Helena with three survivors who had lived on the flesh of their companions.

I went to see Hannah Williams. The inflammatory rheumatism has gone partly out of her legs but her poor hands are now in fiery agonizing pain. She can bear them in almost boiling water. I talked to her very seriously about her past wild conduct since her Confirmation, and prayed with her. Then I read her the May Queen, New Year's Eve, the Conclusion, the Miller's Daughter, and St Agnes Eve, hoping to read her to sleep, but in vain.

I met the doctor (Mr Spencer) here this morning. He told me he had feared at first inflammation of the spinal cord which might have carried Hannah off in 48 hours.

THURSDAY, NEW YEAR'S EVE

Edwin Law told me of an infallible receipt for warming cold and wet feet on a journey. Pour half a glass of brandy into each boot. Also he often carries a large pair of stockings with him to wear over boots and trousers. He has been a long time in Nova Scotia.

My mother and I sat up by the dining room fire to watch the Old Year out and the New Year in. Soon after eleven o'clock the Chippenham bells began pealing and continued to ring at intervals till after midnight. The wind had veered into the South and brought the sound of the bells to us very distinct and sweet across the river, so that we could plainly hear when they began and paused and all the change-ringing and the firing of the bells. At a quarter to twelve I began to think earnestly of dear Katie and to pray for her. I knew she would be watching, praying and thinking of me. I had laid before me on my desk the photograph of her in her riding habit and the New Year's card I had just received from her. She seemed to be very near me. I felt her love all round me and I was very happy. My last thoughts and prayers in the Old Year 1874 were for her.

— 1875 —

FRIDAY, NEW YEAR'S DAY

I went across to Hannah Williams. I had not seen her for two days and there was a brilliant look of glad welcome on the proud beautiful face, as the wistful dark eyes seemed to say, 'Where have you been? I thought you had forgotten me.'

TUESDAY, 12 JANUARY

John Hatherell told me this evening that he recollects when a boy being one of the bearers at the burial of a gipsy girl 12 years of age. He had forgotten her name but we looked in the parish registers and found the entry of the funeral. The girl's name was 'Limpedy Buckland'. She was buried in Langley Burrell Churchyard in the year 1809 on the 29th of April. She died in the tents of her people in Sutton Lane opposite the gate of Sand Furlong. The road was then a green lane. When John and the other lads who were to be bearers reached the tents of the tribe they found a clean white cloth laid upon the green grass with bread, cheese, and beer, and an old woman, the mother or grandmother of the dead girl, put her hand into her pocket and gave each of the bearer lads a shilling. Then the lads carried the girl to her grave and a white sheet was thrown over the coffin. Limpedy Buckland the gipsy girl was buried in the south-eastern corner of the churchyard under the great yew.

Hannah Hatherell said she well remembered old Constant Smith the gipsy. Probably this was 'Constance Smith a gipsy', the mother of 'Muperella' whose burial appears in the registers of Langley Burrell. Hannah also remembers well old Ted Buckland the gipsy who murdered Judy Pearce at the lone house between Sutton and Seagry, since called Murder Cottage on that account. This Ted Buckland used to go about wrapped in a white blanket girt about his waist with a girdle and pinned together over his chest with a skewer. My mother saw him brought to my grandfather's house at Langley Fitzurse after the murder in this same costume.

William Ferris told me to-day his reminiscences of the first train that ever came down the Great Western Railway. 'I was foddering,' he said, 'near the line. It was a hot day in May some 34 or 35 years ago, and I heard a roaring in the air. I looked up and thought there was a storm coming down from Christian Malford roaring in the tops of the trees, only the day was so fine and hot. Well, the roaring came nigher and nigher, then the train shot along and the dust did flee up.'

FRIDAY, 15 JANUARY

Speaking to the children at the school about the Collect
for the 2nd Sunday after the Epiphany and God's peace
I asked them what beautiful image and picture of peace
we have in the xxxiii Psalm. 'The Good Shepherd,' said
I, 'leading His sheep to –?' 'To the slaughter,' said Frederick Herriman promptly. One day I asked the children
to what animal our Saviour is compared in the Bible.
Frank Matthews confidently held out his hand. 'To an
ass,' he said.

SATURDAY, 16 JANUARY

In the Common Field in front of the cottages I found two
little figures in the dusk. One tiny urchin was carefully
binding a handkerchief round the face of an urchin even
more tiny than himself. It was Fred and Jerry Savine.
'What are you doing to him?' I asked Fred. 'Please, Sir,'
said the child solemnly. 'Please, Sir, we'm gwine to play
at blindman's buff.' The two children were quite alone.
The strip of dusky meadow was like a marsh and every
footstep trod the water out of the soaked land, but the
two little images went solemnly on with their game as
if they were in a magnificent playground with a hundred children to play with. Oh, the wealth of a child's
imagination and capacity for enjoyment of trifles.

WEDNESDAY, 20 JANUARY

I went to luncheon to-day at Langley House to meet Mence who came there last Monday. I have not been inside the doors of Langley House since last July, and then I went there unasked to get the Squire's subscription for the cricket club.

THURSDAY, 21 JANUARY

I went round the premises late at night to see if the outhouses were locked up. All was still and the white pig lying in the moonlight at the door of his house, fast asleep, with the moon shining on his white face and round cheek.

SATURDAY, 23 JANUARY

When I went to bed last night I fancied that something ran in at my bedroom door after me from the gallery. It seemed to be a skeleton. It ran with a dancing step and I thought it aimed a blow at me from behind. This was shortly before midnight.

SEPTUAGESIMA SUNDAY, 24 JANUARY

Last night I dreamt I saw a great whale caught in Weymouth Bay. I watched the huge dark bulk heave and tumble in the sea. Then the boats put out with harpoons and lances. The battle raged and drifted out of sight of the dream, but the bay was crimson with blood.

SATURDAY, 30 JANUARY

I dined at Langley House. It is a long time since I dined there, more than a year I think. Syddie was looking lovely. Thersie dined with us and Syddie came in to dessert. The Squire appeared in the drawing room before dinner in a long grey dressing gown, took Mrs Money Kyrle down and dined at a little table by himself, joining however in the talk. Colonel Money Kyrle took the foot of the table. After the ladies had left us we sat before the fire over a bottle of '51 port discussing the Prayer Book Dissenters till nearly 10.30. I took Thersie down to dinner. We had a woodcock which had been shot in the Marsh by the Squire.

TUESDAY, CANDLEMAS DAY

I went to see Benjamin Hawkins. 'The times were much harder for poor folk when I was a lad, let people say what they will,' said Benjamin. Sometimes when an outstanding field rick was threshed or brought into the barn the shepherd or carter had the privilege of planting a few potatoes there and he was so overjoyed with his good fortune that he thought he had got a small farm. There was no such thing known then as planting potatoes in the field, and this made every foot of the garden ground so precious that people could not spare room for flowerbeds. Some of the old women would have a flower border and raise a few pinks and roses and a little thyme and lad's love, make up the flowers into knots and nosegays, and sell them at a halfpenny apiece. The lads would buy them and stick them in their hats on Sundays. Nosegays were very much sought after. Benjamin thought the new law compelling boys to go to school till they are 12 years old a bad law, unjust and hard upon the parents.

FRIDAY, 5 FEBRUARY

My mother tells us that when she was a little child of three or four years old she was sent every morning with a nurse from her father's house at Langley Fitzurse to the village school kept by Dame Fairlamb at the Pound, Langley Burrell, in the cottages where old blind Thomas Jefferies lived and died. My mother was not allowed to play with the village children but when school was over she was taken home by the nurse. Dame Fairlamb was one of the real old fashioned dames, severe and respectable with rod and spectacles. Afterwards my Mother went to the Moravian school at East Tytherton daily on a donkey which she urged forward by rattling a bunch of keys in his ear.

FRIDAY, 12 FEBRUARY

I went to see old Sally Killing. She is very comfortable and contented now sitting in her cosy chimney corner, with Aileen for her lady's maid. Aileen told me of the sad uneven marriage at St Paul's Church, Chippenham, last week, the daughter of the clergyman of [–] married to her father's groom with whom, unknown to her parents, she had been keeping company for *five years*.

But how without her parents' knowledge? The groom's sister made the young lady's dresses and the groom used to drive the young lady to see her dressmaker. A sad story.

SUNDAY, ST VALENTINE'S DAY

Shortly after noon to-day, at the time the folk were coming out of morning Church, the village Patriarch old John Bryant quietly ended his long earthly pilgrimage and passed away from amongst us, we hope and trust to a better country. The old man died very calmly and peacefully like a little child falling asleep. He was baptized July 30th, 1780, but he was probably born in 1779.

MONDAY, ST VALENTINE'S MORROW

The Miss Mascalls were justly indignant and amazed that Mrs Prodgers and her children should have been introduced into the new painted east window in Kington St Michael's Church, 'Suffer little children to come unto me'. Mrs Prodgers and her children actually sat for their likenesses and she is introduced as one of the mothers, in the most prominent position. The whole thing is the laughing stock of the village and countryside.

TUESDAY, 16 FEBRUARY

Miss Bryant told me that her grandmother, Miss Buy of Langley Brewery, asked her grandfather George Bryant to marry her, and bitterly repented it afterwards. George

Bryant was a very fine handsome man and Miss Buy said to him, 'Why do you go courting a woollen apron when you might have a muslim apron?'

THURSDAY, 4 MARCH

Old William Halliday told me he had heard from the old people of Allington and especially from the Taverners, when he was young, strange tales of ancient times and how the world was once full of 'witches, weasels (wizards) and wolves'. Old William also told the story of how old Squire Sadler Gale of Bulwich House at Allington made himself wings and flew off the garden wall. 'Watch I vlee!' he cried to the people. Then he dashed down into the horsepond.

SATURDAY, 6 MARCH

A sudden and blessed change in the weather, a S. W. wind, pouring warm rain, and the birds in the garden and orchard singing like mad creatures, the whole air in a charm and tumult of joy and delight.

THURSDAY, 11 MARCH

It was a fine clear starry night and the young moon was shining brightly. Near the school I overtook a lad of eighteen walking slowly and wearily, who asked me how far it was to Sutton. He said he had walked down to-day from Broad Hinton, 7 miles the other side of Swindon. He was seeking work and could find none. He was very tired, he said, and he seemed downcast and out of spirits. He had just asked the Sutton baker to give him a lift in his trap, promising to give him a pint of beer, but the baker surlily bade him keep his beer to himself and refused to pull up and take the lad in, giving him leave however to hang on behind the trap from Broad Somerford to Seagry. He had tried to get a bed at Somerford but the inn was full of navvies who are making the new railroad to Malmesbury from Dauntesey.

There was no room for him in the inn. I thought it might encourage and cheer the lad up if I kept company along the road to Sutton so we walked together and I showed him the short cut across the fields. As we went we fell into talk and the lad began to be confidential and to tell me something of his story. It was a simple touching tale. 'I was born,' said the lad, 'at a little village near here called Corston, but I have been knocking about the country looking for work. I have some aunts in Corston.' 'But have you no father or mother?' I asked. The simple chance question touched a heart still tender and bruised with a great sorrow and opened the floodgates of his soul. The lad suddenly burst into tears. 'My Mother was buried to-day,' he sobbed. 'I walked up to Broad Hinton yesterday, to try to get work, for my stepfather would not keep me any longer and I could get no work in Corston. I would have stayed to follow my mother to the grave but I had no black clothes except a jacket and couldn't get any. She was the best friend I had in the world and the only one. I was with her when she died. She said I had better die too along with her for I should only be knocked about in a hard world and there would be no one to care for me. And I've found her words true and thought upon them often enough already,' added the poor boy bitterly with another burst of heart-broken tears.

'My name is Henry Estcourt Ferris,' the lad went on, in answer to some questions of mine. 'My father's name is Estcourt. He is a labouring man working in Wales as a boiler maker. He ran away from my Mother and forsook her six months before I was born. My Mother's maiden name,' said the poor boy with some hesitation, 'was Ellen Ferris.' Alas, the old, old story. Trust misplaced, promises broken, temptation, sin and sorrow, and the sins of the parents visited upon the children. When we got to Sutton we went to three places, two inns and a private lodging house, to try to get the lad a bed. A villager in the street told us of the lodging house, but everywhere the lad was refused a bed and from each house in succession he turned wearily and hopelessly away with a faint protest and remonstrance and a lingering request that the good people would please to try if they could not put him up, but in vain, and we plodded on again towards Chippenham where he knew he could get a bed at the Little George. The poor fellow was very humble and grateful. 'I shouldn't have been near so far along the road as this, if it hadn't been for you, Sir,' he said gratefully. 'You've kind of livened and 'ticed me along.' I cheered him up as well as I could and gave him a bit of good advice. He hoped to get a place at Chippenham Great Market to-morrow. The lights of Langley Fitzurse shone brightly through the dark night. ' 'Tis a long road,' said the lad wearily. At the Hillocks stile we parted at length with a clasp of the hand and a kindly 'Goodbye' and I saw the last, for ever probably in this world, of the motherless boy.

FRIDAY, 19 MARCH

I was very much annoyed this evening by a note from Marion Vaughan saying that my last letter to Netta had been forwarded by Matilda to her at the C.D.S. at Bristol, that Miss Winter had opened the letter, read it, refused to give it to Netta, and then laid it before the Committee, and that the Honorary Secretary had written to Mr Vaughan saying that if Netta continued to receive letters from me he must withdraw her from the school.

EASTER TUESDAY, 30 MARCH

As I walked up and down our drive within the white gate in the fresh mild evening shortly before 8 o'clock I saw through the trees a light from the Manor House nearly half a mile away. The light was obscured continually, apparently by the figures passing before it, and it seemed to come from the dining-room where the Squire was at dinner and probably the constant darkening of the light was produced by the maids waiting at table and passing every moment almost between the window and the lights on the table.

WEDNESDAY, APRIL EVE

This evening Teddy left us and went back to London. I walked down with him to the station. He went up by a broad gauge train and in the smoking carriage, the atmosphere of which I could not have endured for a minute and could hardly bear to stand near the door even.

MONDAY, 5 APRIL

Left Langley for Monnington-on-Wye with Dora. William met us at Moorhampton with the dog cart and chestnut horse Paddy, and drove us to Monnington. I like the look of the place very much. The house is large and comfortable and the situation pretty, roomy and pleasant. One great feature of the place is the famous 'Monnington Walk', a noble avenue of magnificent Scotch firs bordering a broad green ride, stretching from Brobury Scar (a red sandstone precipice beetling over the winds of Wye) to Monnington Court House, where the aunt of Owen Glendower lived.

TUESDAY, 6 APRIL

When I awoke a woodpigeon was crooning from the trees near the house and the early morning sunshine glinted upon the red boles of the gigantic Scotch firs in Monnington Walk. I rose early and went out. The morning was fresh and bright with a slight sunshiny shower flying. Hard by the Church porch and on the western side of it I saw what I knew must be the grave of Owen Glendower. It is a flat stone of whitish grey shaped like a rude obelisk figure, sunk deep into the ground in the middle of an oblong patch of earth from which the turf has been pared away, and, alas, smashed into several fragments. And here in the little Herefordshire church-yard within hearing of the rushing of the Wye and close under the shadow of the old grey church the strong wild heart, still now, has rested by the ancient home and roof tree of his kindred since he fell asleep there more than four hundred years ago. It is a quiet peaceful spot.

In the afternoon Thersie, Dora, Florence and I called at Monnington Court and were kindly received by the worthy Churchwarden farmer and his wife, Mr and Mrs James, who showed us the fine old oak carving and the banqueting room. In the garden of the Court House was dug up a few days ago a huge silver coin which Mr James showed us and which looked to me like a crown of Charles I. On one side of the coin was a king crowned, armed and mounted. Mr James went with us to the Church which is light and pleasant and cheerful within and seemed well cared for. He told us that in the great flood of February 6, 1852, he and the present Sir Gilbert Lewis of Harpton (then Rector of Monnington), had punted in a flat-bottomed boat across the Court garden, in at the Church door, up the Nave and into the Chancel.

THURSDAY, 8 APRIL

A sad accident lately befell the poor strange Solitary, the Vicar of Llanbedr Painscastle. He was sitting by the fire in his little lone hut at Cwm Cello that lies in the bosom of Llanbedr Hill when he either dropped heavily asleep or had a fit and fell full upon the fire. Before he could recover himself his stomach, bowels and thighs were dreadfully burnt, and he has had to stay away from Church for three Sundays. Yet he will let neither doctor nor nurse come near him. The poor solitary. He used to visit Sarah Bryan kindly and assiduously when she lay a-dying and was a great and lasting comfort to her. She died very happy.

TUESDAY, 13 APRIL

I had not been in Builth since that memorable day to me, May 29th, 1865, the day never to be forgotten when I walked alone over the hills from Clyro to Builth and first saw the Rocks of Aberedw, the day I first saw Painscastle and the ruined Church of Llanbedr, and the morning sun shining like silver upon Llanbychllyn Pool, and descended from the great moor upon the vale of Edw and saw, in the orchard of the newly yellow-thatched cottage near the Court Mills, the two beautiful chestnut-haired girls at play with the children under the apple boughs. Then every step was through an enchanted land. I was discovering a new country and all the world was before me. How different it is now, just ten years afterwards. But then there was a glamour and enchantment about the first view of the shining slate roofs of Builth and the bridge and the winding reaches of the broad and shining river which even now cling about the place and have never quite been dispelled. A strange fascination, a beautiful enchantment hangs over Builth and the town is magically transfigured still.

Oh, Aberedw, Aberedw. Would God I might dwell and die by thee. Memory enters in and brings back the old time in a clear vision and waking dream, and again I descend from the high moor's half encircling sweep and listen to the distant murmur of the river as it foams down the ravine from its home in the Green Cwm and its cradle in the hills. Once more I stand by the riverside and look up at the cliff castle towers and mark the wild roses swinging from the crag and watch the green woods waving and shimmering with a twinkling dazzle as they rustle in the breeze and shining of the summer afternoon, while here and there a grey crag peeps from among the tufted trees. And once again I hear the merry voices and laughter of the children as they clamber down the cliff path among the bushes or along the rock ledges of the riverside or climb the Castle Mount, or saunter along the narrow green meadow tree-fringed and rock-bordered and pass in and out of Llewellyn's cave, or gather wood and light the fire amongst the rocks upon the moor, or loiter down the valley to Cavan Twm Bach and cross the shining ferry at sunset, when the evening shadows lie long and still across the broad reaches of the river. Oh, Aberedw, Aberedw.

HOLY THURSDAY, 6 MAY

John Couzens says he is very fond of dry bread, as dry and hard as he can get it. 'When I was out mowing,' he said, 'I used to throw my wallet and my victuals on the swath and let the sun *bless it* from bait to bait. I wanted it all crust.'

MONDAY, 24 MAY

This afternoon I walked over to Lanhill. As I came down from the hill into the valley across the golden meadows and along the flower-scented hedges a great wave of emotion and happiness stirred and rose up within me. I know not why I was so happy, nor what I was expecting, but I was in a delirium of joy, it was one of the supreme few moments of existence, a deep delicious draught from the strong sweet cup of life. It came unsought, unbidden, at the meadow stile, it was one of the flowers of happiness scattered for us and found unexpectedly by the wayside of life. It came silently, suddenly, and it went as it came, but it left a long lingering glow and glory behind as it faded slowly like a gorgeous sunset, and I shall ever remember the place and the time in which such great happiness fell upon me.

THURSDAY, 27 MAY

My bedroom is illuminated all day with a beautiful rosy light from the glorious blossom of the pink may on the lawn.

WEDNESDAY, JUNE MORROW

Austin told me that when his present farm boy, Robert Jefferies, worked at the Barrow the young Bryants held him down in the furrow and ploughed him into the ground. It reminded me of Uncle Francis trying to bury Uncle Richard when they were boys at Caroline Buildings in

Bath. He had got him into the hole up to his waist when someone came by and interrupted him. In a fury he flung the spade at Richard to cut him in two and finish him at once, but the spade fell on his own foot and Francis swore like a trooper.

FRIDAY, 4 JUNE

Mrs Vincent told me that her husband had not suffered so much lately from the pressure of water upon his heart which had been sensibly relieved by the water running out at his heels.

MONDAY, 7 JUNE

I walked to Langley Grove through the mowing grass. Dear little Katie opened the door to me and her father Farmer Lessiter was better and sitting downstairs at tea. When I went away and shook hands with him at parting he gave me a kind look out of his blue eyes and said, 'I wish I were as strong as you, Sir. I know you must be a very strong man. When I was in bed the other day and you shook hands with me I felt as if an electrifying machine had gone all through me and I feel the same now. I made the remark after you were gone that you must be a very strong man. There is something so stiff to lean against in your grasp.'

'Oh,' I said, 'you will be as strong as I am again in a few days.'

'No,' said the stout farmer, with a sad shake of the

head and a sorrowful look in his blue eyes. 'No, I shall never be as strong as you are any more.'

TUESDAY, 8 JUNE

How delightful it is in these sweet summer evenings to wander from cottage to cottage and from farm to farm exchanging bright words and looks with the beautiful girls at their garden gates and talking to the kindly people sitting at their cottage doors or meeting in the lane when their work is done. How sweet it is to pass from house to house welcome and beloved everywhere by young and old, to meet the happy loving smiles of the dear children at their evening play in the lanes and fields and to meet with no harsher reproach than this, 'It is a longful while since you have been to see us. We do all love to see you coming and we do miss you sorely when you are away.'

SATURDAY, 12 JUNE

I went to see my dear little lover Mary Tavener, the deaf and half dumb child. When I opened the door of the poor old crazy cottage in the yard the girl uttered a passionate inarticulate cry of joy and running to me she flung her arms round my neck and covered me with kisses. Well, I have lived and I have been loved, and no one can take this from me.

FRIDAY, 18 JUNE

Battle of Waterloo. ''Tis sixty years since.' The veterans who meet at the yearly banquet must be growing very few and feeble. It must be a small sad gathering now, and soon there will be fewer and then there will be none.

I passed by the ruined sheds which sadly, regretfully, mark the site of the ancient small homestead of Watling Street. The dwelling house has entirely disappeared and the scene of so many joys and sorrows, hopes and fears, is now waste, silent and desolate, and overgrown with nettles and weeds. What a pity that these ancient humble farms should be destroyed and thrown into the great farms, thereby taking away all the poor man's prizes and the chance of his rising in the world.

TUESDAY, 22 JUNE

I have been working all the afternoon in our meadows with the haymakers, Farmer Jacob Knight, John Couzens, Hannah, Mary and Joseph Hatherell and Emma Halliday. We have got a lot of beautiful green fragment hay up in cock.

WEDNESDAY, MIDSUMMER EVE

Another beautiful haymaking day. We all worked hard and got the hay up in beautiful condition, I pitching the last four loads with Jacob Knight. We finished about nine o'clock of a lovely warm Midsummer's Eve.

THURSDAY, MIDSUMMER DAY

And a lovely day it has been, soft, warm and sunny. I took the young cuckoo out of his nest, put him in the great wicker cage, and hung the cage up in the hawthorn hedge close to the old nest that the hedge sparrows might feed their charge.

Gathering strawberries. As the day wore the weather became more and more beautiful till at last the evening grew the loveliest I think I ever saw. The rich golden light flooded the lawn and clean freshly cleared meadows, slanting through the western trees which fringe the Common's edge. Even the roan cows, and the Alderney especially, glowed with a golden tinge in the glorious evening sunlight. From the wide common over the thick waving fragrant grass came the sweet country music of the white-sleeved mowers whetting their scythes and the voices of their children at play among the fresh-cut flowery swaths. The sun went down red under a delicate fringe of gold laced cloud, the beautiful Midsummer evening passed through twilight and gloaming into the exquisite warm soft Midsummer night, with its long light in the north slowly, softly lingering as Jupiter came out glorious in the south and flashed glittering through the tresses of the silver birches softly waving, and the high poplars rustled whispering and the Church clock at Draycot struck ten and I longed to sleep out of doors and dream my 'Midsummer night's dream'.

MONDAY, 24 JUNE

Villaging. Visited Mrs Lawrence who amused me by a description of how she fell down the cellar stairs from top to bottom by reason of her 'grasping on vacancy' instead of grasping a pound of candles which were hanging against the wall. When she revived herself and came up, 'Charles,' she said to her husband, 'I am almost dead. I have fallen from the top of the cellar stairs to the bottom.' 'You couldn't have done it,' said Charles incredulously from under the bedclothes. 'I *have* done it, Charles,' she shouted, infuriated at his unbelief.

MONDAY, 5 JULY

Left Chippenham for the Isle of Wight. Reached Shanklin between 4 and 5 o'clock, the heat all the way very great in the sun in spite of a fine breeze. It was most refreshing and delightful embarking in the steam boat with the salt air blowing cool, the sea dimpling, sparkling and shimmering, the Island smiling in the glorious afternoon sunlight and the tall white-sailed yachts standing stately up and down the Solent and flying over the bright blue water.

WEDNESDAY, 7 JULY

At 5 o'clock we all went down to the beach leaving Mrs Cowper Coles in her Bath Chair on the top of the Cliff. Mrs Powles, Miss Deason, Gussie and Alice sat down by the bathing machine to sketch Sampson's Cottage at the mouth of the Chine. Minna, Sherard, Commerell, Cowper Todd and I set to work to dig sand castles and trenches. The tide was going out, a number of children were paddling in the shallow water left by the white retreating surges, and it was a fair sight to watch the merry girls with their pretty white feet and bare limbs wading through the little rippling waves or walking on the wet and shining sand. Oh, as I watched them there came over me such a longing, such a hungry yearning to have one of those children for my own. Oh that I too had a child to love and to love me, a daughter with such fair limbs and blue eyes archly dancing, and bright clustering curls blown wild and golden in the sunshine and sea air. It came over me like a storm and I turned away hungry at heart and half envying the parents as they sat upon the sand watching their children at play.

TUESDAY, 13 JULY

This morning after breakfast I started to walk to Bembridge through Sandown and Yaverland. The morning was blue and lovely with a warm sun and fresh breeze blowing from the sea and the Culver Downs. As I walked from Shanklin to Sandown along the cliff edge I stopped to watch some children bathing from the beach directly below. One beautiful girl stood entirely naked on the sand, and there as she half sat, half reclined sideways, leaning upon her elbow with her knees bent and her legs and feet partly drawn back and up, she was a model for a sculptor, there was the supple slender waist, the gentle dawn and tender swell of the bosom and the budding breasts, the graceful rounding of the delicately beautiful limbs and above all the soft and exquisite curves of the rosy dimpled bottom and broad white thigh. Her dark hair fell in thick masses on her white shoulders as she threw her head back and looked out to sea. She seemed a Venus Anadyomene fresh risen from the waves.

I missed the road by the windmill on the height and went too far round to the right, but at last returning by the Cross Roads I came to Bembridge. Bosomed amongst green, pretty cottages peeped through the thick foliage and here and there a garden shone brilliant with flowers. A long beautiful road, dark, green and cool and completely overarched with trees, led towards the sea and in a high meadow the haymakers in their white shirt sleeves, the dark horses and the high loaded waggon stood out clear against the brilliant blue waters of the Channel. Farther on a broad and beautiful avenue led down to the water's edge. The trees were chiefly sycamore and ash, and high and thickly over-arching they cast a twinkling chequering shadow upon the ground, a perpetual restless flicker of dancing leaves that in the sun and sea wind moved ceaselessly quivering. Only two or three children were moving up and down in the chequering sunlight and shadow. At the end of the avenue the bright blue sea was framed in a perfect round low arch of dark foliage, and passing under the arch I came out upon an open terrace from which a pretty winding path wandered amongst the woods which fringe the shore and sweep down to the water's edge. Spithead was full of great ships black and monstrous. The Channel

Fleet had come in the day before and was lying off the opposite shore. The sun shone bright on the green slopes and woods and white houses of St Helens across the smooth blue harbour of Brading, a woman sat solitary under the trees looking across the sea to the Hampshire coast, and the only sound that broke the peaceful stillness were the rustling of the firs and poplars overhead and the clapping of the white sail of a pilot boat as it flapped idly from the yard in the soft sea breeze.

[Kilvert returns to Langley Burrell.]

MONDAY, 19 JULY

I called on Mrs Martin. She was busy picking pheasants' feathers to make a pillow. Talking of feather beds she said, 'Pheasants' feathers will do very well for a bed, but not pigeons' feathers. People don't like to sleep on pigeons' feathers.' 'Why not?' I asked. 'Well,' said Susan Martin mysteriously, 'folk do say that a person can't die on pigeons' feathers.'

At 7 o'clock came on another terrible storm of rain much worse than the one in the afternoon. I was in my room reading when I heard Fanny screaming to me from the top of the house. Rushing up the back stairs I found that the cistern was overflowing and deluging the water closet, the tank room, and the bathroom and the kitchen. I was obliged to put on a mackintosh and stand in the water closet holding up the handle to relieve the cistern while the water ran down upon my head like a shower bath.

SATURDAY, 24 JULY

Going into the Churchyard I found they were beginning the restoration of Chippenham Church and digging the foundations for the new North aisle. Draper Wharry's assistant at the Chemist's shop told me that things were not managed nicely when the tombstones and graves were necessarily interfered with. He said scalps with hair still on them were left lying about and that he himself had seen a hedgehog tearing at the arm of a body which still had flesh upon it.

TUESDAY, 10 AUGUST

At the Barrow Cottages I found Alice Couzens at home and Charlotte Knight told me the sad story of Mrs Sarten's confinement, how the doctors could not get the dead baby from her for two days and were obliged to cut the poor girl almost to pieces. They said she would die in two hours but she still lives and it is hoped will live, as she has survived a fortnight.

THURSDAY, 12 AUGUST

I walked across to Kington St Michael to be present at the school feast. As we were swinging the children under the elms that crown the Tor Hill a girl came up to me with a beseeching look in her eyes and an irresistible request for a swing. She was a perfect little beauty with a plump rosy face, dark hair, and lovely soft dark eyes melting with tenderness and a sweet little mouth as pretty as a rosebud. I lifted her into the swing and away she went. But about the sixth flight the girl suddenly slipped off the swing seat feet foremost and still keeping hold of the ropes she hung from the swing helpless. Unfortunately her clothes had got hitched upon the seat of the swing and were all pulled up round her waist and it instantly became apparent that she wore no drawers. A titter and then a shout of laughter ran through the crowd as the girl's plump person was seen naked hanging from the swing. O ye gods, the fall of Hebe was nothing to it. We hustled her out of the swing and her clothes into their proper place as soon as possible and perhaps she did not know what a spectacle she had presented. I believe it was partly my fault. When I lifted the girl into the swing there were many aspirants for the seat and in the struggle and confusion I suppose I set her down with her clothes rumpled up and her bare flesh (poor child) upon the board and as her flesh was plump and smooth and in excellent whipping condition and the board slippery, they managed to part company with this result. Poor child, when she begged so earnestly for a swing she scarcely contemplated the exhibition of herself for the amusement of the spectators. I shall never see the elms on the Tor Hill now without thinking of the fall of Hebe.

THURSDAY, 19 AUGUST

In the newspapers this morning we saw the account of the Royal yacht the *Alberta* with the Queen on board going from Osborne to Portsmouth running down, cutting in two and sinking Mr Heywood's yacht the *Mistletoe* in Stokes Bay with a loss of three lives, the master, the mate and Miss Annie Peel, the sister of Mrs Heywood. This is the first accident that has ever happened to the Queen in travelling and she is terribly distressed. It is an awkward thing for the Sovereign to destroy her own subjects. Of course it was no fault of hers but the Royal yacht was travelling too fast through the crowded waters of the Solent.

WEDNESDAY, 25 AUGUST

I went to Britford Vicarage to stay with the Morrises till Saturday. Late in the evening we loitered down into the water meads. The sun was setting in stormy splendour behind Salisbury and the marvellous aerial spire rose against the yellow glare like Ithuriel's spear, while the last gleams of the sunset flamed down the long lines of the water carriages making them shine and glow like canals of molten gold.

FRIDAY, 27 AUGUST

To-day I paid my first visit to Stonehenge. We had breakfast before Church and immediately after service Morris and I started to walk to Stonehenge, eleven miles. Passing through the beautiful Cathedral Close and the city of Salisbury we took the Devizes road and after we had walked along that road for some six miles we saw in the dim distance the mysterious Stones standing upon the Plain. The sun was hot, but a sweet soft air moved over the Plain 'wafting' the scent of the purple heather tufts and the beds of thyme and making the delicate blue harebells tremble on their fragile stems. A beautiful little wheatear flitted before us from one stone heap to another along the side of the wheel track as we struck across the firm elastic turf. Around us the Plain heaved mournfully with great and solemn barrows, the 'grassy barrows of the happier dead'.

Soon after we left the Druid's Head and struck across the turf eastward we came in sight of the grey cluster of gigantic Stones. They stood in the midst of a green plain, and the first impression they left on my mind was that of a group of people standing about and talking together. It seemed to me as if they were ancient giants who suddenly became silent and stiffened into stone directly anyone approached, but who might at any moment become alive again, and at certain seasons, as at midnight and on Old Christmas and Midsummers Eve, might form a true 'Chorea Gigantum' and circle on the Plain in a solemn and stately dance. It is a solemn awful place. As I entered the charmed circle of the sombre Stones I instinctively uncovered my head. It was like entering a great Cathedral Church.

Crossing the river at Normanton Hatches we walked along the hillside through meadows and barley fields till we came to the hospitable Manor House of Great Durnford, the seat of Mr John Pinckney, where we found Mr and Mrs Pinckney, Mr Charles Everett and Major Fisher, the Champion archer of England, at luncheon. After luncheon the archers went out to shoot at a beautiful archery ground by the riverside. The ladies sat watching under the trees while the arrows flashed past with a whistling rush, and the glorious afternoon sunlight shone mellow upon the beeches, and the still soft air of the river valley was filled with the cooing of woodpigeons and the strange mournful crying of the moorhens and dabchicks, and three beautiful cows came down the glade from sunlight to shadow to their milking place, and the river flashed darkly past the boathouse and under the leaning trees, and a man rowed up the stream with his milkcans in a boat from the meadows where he had milked a distant herd of cows.

SATURDAY, 28 AUGUST

Left Britford, came home in pouring rain.

William Boscawen told us of a curious custom which is still kept up in many parts of Wales. At the funerals offerings are made at the graveside to the clergyman by the mourners and the offerings are collected upon the grave shovel. This is a relic of the old Catholic custom of offering money to the priest to say masses for the soul of the departed.

He said that an old woman who had lately moved from her parish into an adjoining one died there. Soon afterwards meeting the husband Boscawen inquired about her last days, and received the following account. 'Hun did send for the parson.' 'Well?' 'And hun did come and say that hun must repent of her sins. 'Yes.' 'And hun did say as hun hadn't got any sins to repent of.' 'Well?' 'Then hun did say that as if hun hadn't got any sins hun shouldn't come to see hun any more.' 'Well?' 'Hun didn't come.' 'And then?' 'Hun died.'

SUNDAY, 29 AUGUST

John Hatherell told me that one night he had a sweet waking dream. He thought one of his children was with him and sitting on his bed. It was Ellen. And he said to her that he wanted to kiss Some One. 'Kiss me, father,' said Ellen. But he did not mean that. There seemed to be Some One else there whom he was feeling after. 'It was my sweet Jesus that I wanted to kiss,' said the old man.

SATURDAY, 4 SEPTEMBER

This beautiful autumn morning I went out to pray on the sunny common. The luxuriant meadow grass shone green and silver with the hoary webs and sheets of dew. The hills and woods and distances were richly bloomed with azure misty veils, the sweet sudden solitary song of the robin from the hornbeam broke the morning calm, and here and there a yellow leaf, the herald of Autumn, floated silently from the limes.

Dora and I drove to Seagry Vicarage to luncheon and to go nutting with the Charles Awdrys' children in Seagry. We had a grand scramble and merry romp in the Seagry Woods racing up and down the green rides, clambering over the high gates gathering nuts, throwing burrs at each other and sticking them in the girls' hair amidst shouts and screams of laughter.

MONDAY, 6 SEPTEMBER

All night the heavy drenching fog brooded over the land, clinging to the meadows long after the sun was risen, and it was not until after he had gained some height in the sky that he was able to break through and dispel the mists. Then the morning suddenly became glorious and we saw what had happened in the night. All night long millions of gossamer spiders had been spinning and the whole country was covered as if with one vast fairy web. They spread over lawn and meadow grass and gate and hawthorn hedge, and as the morning sun glinted upon their delicate threads drenched and beaded with the film of the mist the gossamer webs gleamed and twinkled into crimson and gold and green, like the most exquisite shot-silk dress in the finest texture of gauzy silver wire. I never saw anything like it or anything so exquisite as 'the Virgin's webs' glowed with changing opal lights and glanced with all the colours of the rainbow.

At 4 o'clock Miss Meredith Brown and her beautiful sister Etty came over to afternoon tea with us and a game of croquet. Etty Meredith Brown is one of the most striking-looking and handsomest girls whom I have seen for a long time. She was admirably dressed in light grey with a close fitting crimson body which set off her exquisite figure and suited to perfection her black hair and eyes and her dark Spanish brunette complexion with its rich glow of health which gave her cheeks the dusky bloom and flush of a ripe pomegranate. But the greatest triumph was her hat, broad and picturesque, carelessly twined with flowers and set jauntily on one side of her pretty dark head, while round her shapely slender throat she wore a rich gold chain necklace with broad gold links. And from beneath the shadow of the picturesque hat the beautiful dark face and the dark wild fine eyes looked with a true gipsy beauty.

The sun shone golden on the lawn between the lengthening shadows and the evening sunlight dappled with bright green on the front of the Rectory with rick spots of light and shade. It lighted the broad gold links of the necklace and the graceful crimson figure of the dark handsome girl, and into the midst of the game came the tabby cat carrying in her mouth her tabby kitten which she dropped on the lawn and looked round proudly for applause.

TUESDAY, 7 SEPTEMBER

This morning I went to Bath. Having an hour to spare I went into the Catholic Cathedral. I knelt and prayed for charity, unity, and brotherly love, and the union of Christendom. Surely a Protestant may pray in a Catholic Church and be none the worse.